Also in the *Lesser Known G*
written by Steve Rob

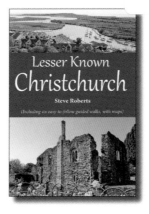

'This well-researched book will tell you things that you will probably not have known about Christchurch and its history. Of interest to visitors to the town as well as residents who may want to explore parts of the borough they don't get to see very often. Dip into any part of this book to find a fascinating fact that will whet your appetite to know more about the town and some of its more colourful historical figures.'

Allan Wood, Communications Officer,
Christchurch and East Dorset Councils

'... unbelievably comprehensive. ... It is inconceivable to think that there is anything you might want to know about the town, its history and things to do that are not covered in some way by it.'

Dorset Life

'... an informative, imaginative and well-researched book about Christchurch. It's a great read and would suit residents and visitors alike, so buy it, read it, and share in the author's love for a town that sounds well worth visiting.'

Amazon review

The Royal Arcade, Boscombe.

Lesser Known
Bournemouth

Steve Roberts

Roving
Press

© 2020 Steve Roberts

Published by Roving Press Ltd
4 Southover Cottages, Frampton, Dorset, DT2 9NQ, UK
Tel: +44 (0)1300 321531
www.rovingpress.co.uk

First published 2020 by Roving Press Ltd

ISBN: 978-1-906651-336

British Library Cataloguing in Publication Data
A catalogue record for this book is available from the British Library.

Cover design by Tim Musk

Maps based on OpenStreet Map © OpenStreetMap contributors.

Set in 11.5/13 pt by Beamreach (www.beamreachuk.co.uk).
Printed and bound by Henry Ling Ltd., at the Dorset Press, Dorchester, DT1 1HD.

Contents

Preface and Acknowledgements   *ix*

Area map   *x*

Introduction   **1**

A Brief History   **8**

Rivers and Seafront   **22**

Gardens and Nature Areas   **32**
Gardens   32
Historic Parks   37
Other Public Open Spaces and Nature Reserves   38
    Central Bournemouth and the West Cliff   38
    Boscombe and Southbourne   39
    North Bournemouth   42
    Littledown, Iford and Tuckton   43
    Hengistbury Head/Solent Meads and Wick Fields   44

The Arts   **46**
A History of Art and Artists in the Area   46
The Art Scene Today   47
Books and Authors   48
Travel Literature   55
Music   56
Dance and Drama   59
Film and TV   62

Folklore and Characters   **65**
Things that Go 'Bump'   65
    Creatures   66
    Murders and Deaths   67
    Characters   68
    Other Oddities   70

Family Fun and Other Activities   **71**
Boating and Ferries   71
Bournemouth Aviary   71
Pier Approach – Big Wheel and Aquarium   72
City Sightseeing Bournemouth   72
Land Trains   72
Miniature Railway   73
Play Areas   73
Youth Centres and Groups   75
Bournemouth Pier   76

Sport and Leisure   **78**

   Water Sports   78
   Fishing   79
   Football   80
   Cricket   82
   Golf   83
   Bowls and Pétanque (French Boules)   84
   Tennis, Squash and Racketball   85
   Athletics   86
   Cycling and BMX   86
   Swimming and Water Polo   87
   Shooting, Archery and Darts   88
   Rugby Union   88
   Hockey   88
   Baseball   88
   Boxing and Wrestling   88
   Ice Skating and Roller Skating   89
   Some that Have Been and Gone   89
   Leisure Centres   90

Regular Events   **92**

Interesting Buildings and Businesses   **97**

   Department Stores   97
   Railway Stations   99
   Churches   100
   Hotels   104
   Brompton Court   106
   Town Hall   106
   The Pavilion   107
   The Opera House, Boscombe
      (now the O2 Academy Bournemouth)   108
   Russell-Cotes House, Gallery and Garden   108
   Other Interesting Buildings   110
   Bournemouth Natural Science Society   110
   The Knole Freemasons' Hall (Walk 5 map)   111
   Boxer Rocket Shed (Walk 6 map)   111
   Lansdowne College (Walk 2)   111
   Original 1952 Listed Domestic Buildings   112
   Architects   112

Exploring   **113**

  Walk 1: Town Centre   115

  Walk 2: East Cliff and Lansdowne   129

  Walk 3: Chines and West Cliff   137

  Walk 4: Westbourne   147

  Walk 5: Boscombe   155

  Walk 6: Wick and Tuckton, and Hengistbury Head   163

  Walk 7: Muscliff, Throop and Holdenhurst   175

  Other Walks and Cycling Routes   184

Some Outlying Areas of the Borough   **186**

  Boscombe and Springbourne   186

  Charminster, Strouden Park and Queens Park   186

  Iford and Tuckton – see Walk 6   187

  Kinson   188

  Littledown   189

  Muscliff, Throop and Holdenhurst – see Walk 7   190

  Ensbury and Redhill   190

  Pokesdown   191

  Southbourne   192

  Talbot Woods   193

  Westbourne – see Walk 4   193

  Wick and Hengistbury Head – see Walk 6   193

  Winton and Moordown   194

Help and Information   **196**

  Maps   196

  Tourist Information Centre   196

  Transport   196

  Russell-Cotes Art Gallery and Museum   197

  Bournemouth Library   197

  Lifeguards   197

Bournemouth's Plaques   **198**

Bibliography   *200*

About the Author   *203*

Some other books by Roving Press   *204*

Index   *207*

Never say see Naples and die; rather say see Bournemouth and live!
(Merton Russell-Cotes, 1835–1921)

The story of Bournemouth is not a history, but a romance.
(Rev. Telford Varley, c 1866–1938)

Bournemouth is one of the few English towns that one can safely call 'her'.
(John Betjeman, 1906–1984)

A Mediterranean lounging place on the English Channel.
(Thomas Hardy, 1840–1928)

The Bournemouth Echo *building on Albert Road, built 1932.*

Preface

This book is part of a series of *Lesser Known* guides published by Roving Press, looking at Dorset towns. Having authored *Lesser Known Christchurch* (2015), I was delighted to be asked to write this new book, as I lived in Bournemouth between 1986 and 1998 and talk about the town in my guise as a public speaker. I also wanted to write a book looking at the whole borough, as there is a lot more to Bournemouth than simply its town centre. For instance, Bournemouth has 21 nature conservation areas, helping provide protection to the area.

Bournemouth is a place with hidden treasures, surprising history and stories awaiting discovery. It is a sad truism that we often overlook what is on our doorstep, so this book will appeal to both residents, wishing to know more about their town, and visitors. As well as descriptions of places, people and events that make Bournemouth special, there are contributions from those living and working here. There are also seven walks to help you explore. Many of the places mentioned in the text are featured in the walks and shown on the respective maps, which I hope will be a useful aid to discovering the town.

Steve Roberts

Acknowledgements

Thanks to everyone who contributed, including those who provided personal stories. The author is grateful to Philip Proctor for his feedback. The author would also like to acknowledge the efforts of all those local historians who have gone before him, who made his life so much easier. While many people were consulted in the writing of this book, any errors are the author's alone. Above all, thanks to the author's inspirational wife Val, who always maintained he had a book in him. Well, here is number two, sweetheart!

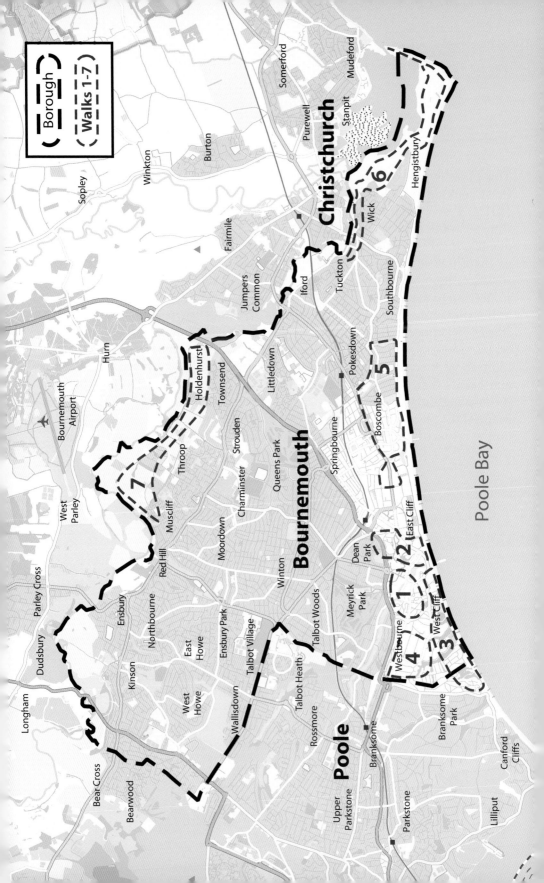

Introduction

Having authored *Lesser Known Christchurch*, I embarked on this latest project with a spring in my step. I knew what I had to do. That jauntiness was soon arrested, however, when I thought more deeply about my subject. Bournemouth is a much bigger place. If we consider just its population, we are talking about a town over four times the size of Christchurch. So many stories, so little space to tell them.

One of the oft-repeated fallacies about Bournemouth is that it has no history, but you only have to consider Hengistbury Head to know this is not so. Of course, it does depend on what we mean by 'Bournemouth'. Geographically, it was a very small place, based around the mouth of the Bourne stream. In 1810, Captain Lewis Tregonwell, a Dorset Ranger in the Corps of Light Infantry, who patrolled Poole Bay looking out for both invaders and smugglers, built a house called The Mansion (now the Royal Exeter Hotel) in Exeter Road and further holiday villas, thus endowing himself with

The mouth of the Bourne at Pier Approach.

1

the name of 'founder of Bournemouth'. But the town didn't really begin its expansion until 1876 when Boscombe and Springbourne were added to the fold. Thus the 'modern' resort has only just over two centuries of history, but it has certainly packed a lot into that relatively short time.

Bournemouth has not only grown, but also changed. When it was first conceived and developed, it was as a place of convalescence for 'invalids' and therefore lacked 'entertainments'. It has successfully reinvented itself, however, and is now one of the UK's leading all-year holiday resorts. The intrinsic belief that Bournemouth is a place for the elderly and infirm has been shed; there is a vibrant night life here now, with a good-sized student population.

The seafront has seen dramatic alterations, not all appreciated by residents or visitors, and the burden of responsibility on councillors to get it right is a heavy one. However, the way buildings become redundant and then find a new *raison d'être* can be fascinating. For instance, Bournemouth's Central Fire Station in Holdenhurst Road was opened in 1902, initially 'home' to two professional firemen, a station foreman and coachman (they had horse-drawn appliances). An upgrade, completed in 1937, bestowed a modern fire station housing four engines and accommodating eight men. The building is Grade II Listed, with its typical Edwardian architecture and original features such as the stone façade, weather-vane and 47-ft brass fireman's pole, which was the longest in the British Fire Service. Following closure of the fire station, the building re-opened as an event venue in 1994. Sam Cox is the manager there.

'The building is owned by Bournemouth University and rented by the Students' Union. We regard ourselves as an old-fashioned night club and live music venue. It's known throughout the student world and is rare, as it's on a main street and not a campus. We certainly punch above our weight. We get touring bands and soloists appear, sometimes when they are on the cusp of making it, such as Rag'n'Bone Man. We also get groups wanting to do a "secret gig" before touring (Duran Duran once did this). Ed Sheeran has played here a couple of times and we've had Blur in for an after-show party. The Subways played here, with the gig appearing in the feature film RocknRolla. *Director Guy Ritchie was in the club. Friday night is our student-only night, with Saturday being open to the general public. We're not just about music though. We also do a comedy night, normally a Wednesday, and have had Rufus Hound appear. Even Graham Norton cut his teeth here.*

We aim to provide different events for different sections, so we won't always have the same crowd in here. The Bournemouth demographic has changed and there is a large bulge in the 20–30 age-group now, with media and design companies attracting younger people, plus the University is a major factor, with 3000 students within a 3-minute walk. We're busiest between September and May/June as we cater for the student year. We've also had the Engine Room open as a café during the day. If you look carefully you'll see that the floor in here

slopes towards the road; that was to help the horses haul the heavy equipment out in the old days!'

Tourism is a massive contributor to Bournemouth today, and 95% of the town's workforce is employed in the service sector. People gravitate here for different reasons. Some, no doubt, are enthused by Bournemouth's 200 or more Listed buildings, others by the fact that it was the first seaside in the UK to secure a Green Tourism award. The town was awarded a Purple Flag in 2010 for providing a wide variety of night-time activities while maintaining the safety of both residents and visitors. 'Sunny, sunny Bournemouth' is a familiar refrain from Cherries football fans at the Vitality Stadium. So just how important is the weather to a town like Bournemouth? Jon Weaver, Head of Resort Marketing and Events Bournemouth and Poole Tourism, explains:

'As one of the UK's top seaside destinations, Bournemouth is open for business all year and is busy 75–80% of the time. While the quietest time is January and February, the town is always vibrant, with lots going on for the many visitors. The peak for holidaymakers is obviously July and August; however, the conference, business and educational sector (English language schools, colleges and university) keep the town busy throughout the year. … Christmas is becoming a much busier time of year for the resort, where we have in the past offered major attractions including an outdoor ice rink in the Lower Gardens and a big-wheel on the seafront. …

We often forget what a great place and unique location Bournemouth is to put on events. When we held the first Air Festival in 2008, we thought only 100,000 visitors would attend and ended up with almost 750,000! We believe we have the best of everything here. We never forget the importance of Bournemouth's origins (the genteel spa feel amidst the pine trees in the chines and Gardens, with miles of sandy beaches and cliffs). Added to this, we animate the town, with lots of events, a range of attractions and places to eat, that millions of visitors now enjoy and experience. As for the dependence on the weather, well this is not your traditional seaside offering, so we've been able to maintain our position and more. In any case, it's always sunny in Bournemouth!'

Shopping is important to the town's economy. Castlepoint's predecessor, the Hampshire Centre, which was opened in 1968 by 'OXO' couple 'Katie' (Mary Holland) and 'Philip' (Richard Clarke), was only the third of its kind and also the largest at the time. The town centre, while it has lost some flagship stores, still has the likes of Beales, referred to by one writer as 'the Harrods of Wessex'.

But Bournemouth is not just about shopping, sunshine, sand and *Shangri-La*. It is something of a cultural icon; check out 'The Arts' chapter for the bewildering array of luminaries who have shared some association with the town. Academia still prevails. The Dorset Institute of Higher Education (1976) became Bournemouth University in 1992, and has almost 20,000

The clock, suspended from the canopy in the pedestrianised Old Christchurch Road, was presented to Bournemouth by Lucerne when the towns twinned in 1981.

students today, albeit its principal campus is just in the borough of Poole. Arts University Bournemouth (AUB) has received gold in Teaching Excellence Framework (TEF) rankings. Bournemouth, twinned with Lucerne (Switzerland) and Netanya (Israel), looks beyond itself.

The two-dozen or so English Language schools have added youthfulness and diversity to the town since students arrived in the 1950s. They provide a hefty boost to the local economy, as international education is worth over £300 million to Bournemouth per annum – the town's second most important earner after tourism. Guido Schillig is Managing Director of the Anglo-Continental School of English (ACSE).

'My Swiss father appreciated the need for English and came to this country to learn it. He actually stayed with a host family in Christchurch and ended up marrying their daughter! He thought he could run his own English Language school and opened his first one in Christchurch in 1950 with a few students from Switzerland. The school moved to its current Wimborne Road site in Bournemouth in 1955. My father was in right at the start before there was much in the way of rules and regulations and it was 10–15 years before the other schools began arriving. Today, Bournemouth is the UK's number-one choice outside London for learning English. We have agents from across the world visit us on familiarisation trips, so the colleges do a good job in promoting both Bournemouth and Poole and undoubtedly provide a beneficial "economic ripple" to the local area. Our college alone has 1250 students in the summer peak, with 400 off-peak. In 2016 we had 68 different nationalities here!

Young students are our "bread and butter"; however, we also run specialist courses, for example, we run an Aviation English division, with tests approved by the Civil Aviation Authority for pilots and air traffic controllers. Since inception, over 400,000 students have passed through ACSE. We're also a significant employer, with over 100 staff (teachers and administrative) on average. Over 70 of our past teachers have gone on to write EFL (English as a Foreign Language) textbooks. We have phenomenal host families here too, who I must pay tribute to. Some of them have been looking after our students for 40 years and enduring relationships have been formed. Our students go on to create their own companies and instinctively think of both Britain and Bournemouth when they set up.'

Bournemouth International Centre (BIC), a large conference, exhibition centre and music venue, opened in August 1984, when singer Johnny Mathis led the way. It attracts top acts from around the world, including singers of the calibre of Dame Shirley Bassey and Sir Tom Jones, sports such as motocross, and the wonderful Lipizzaner Stallions, as well as lucrative party political conferences. BH Live, a social enterprise and leading operator of leisure and event venues, has managed the BIC and Bournemouth Pavilion since 2010 in partnership with the council. Divisional General Manager Steve Turner oversees the BIC.

'Bournemouth International Centre is an important venue in the town, both from a leisure and business perspective. We've had massive pop groups here (e.g. Oasis and Take That), and that will continue, but we never rest on our laurels, and constantly adapt to changing trends; for example, comedy is the new rock, and we've had stand-ups of the highest order (e.g. Michael McIntyre, John Bishop and Lee Evans) who now sell out the main hall. I wonder whether people needed cheering up after the last recession! Our entertainments officers, who assist me in getting the programme right, are a mix of ages and interests, so hopefully between us we get our offering right. We host lots of conferences and exhibitions here too, of course, and it was here in Bournemouth that John Prescott acquired his nickname 'Two Jags'! The local economy benefits inordinately from the venue, an example being the Cheerleading Event in 2019 (Future Cheer) which brought 30,000 people into the town. This is just one illustration of the beneficial impact Bournemouth International Centre has on the region, contributing around £70 million per annum to the local economy through business and cultural tourism.'

Perhaps all this contributed to Bournemouth being voted the happiest place to live in the whole of the UK in 2007 (according to a survey by First Direct). The town saw the second-biggest rise (11.7%) in property prices in the UK in 2017, eclipsed only by Cheltenham. In the same year, its pier and beach was named among the 20 best views in the UK (according to a *Daily Mail* poll). Best Western, the hotel chain, commissioned a survey in 2019 to find the UK's favourite seaside destination and Bournemouth came first (second place fell to Weymouth). The founding fathers may have struggled with one of its modern tag-lines as 'Dorset's nightclub capital', which may (or may not) have some connection to it becoming the first local authority to have CCTV in 1985. Some things do remain the same though and Bournemouth is still a 'town' despite its size (over 180,000 in 2011), an attempt to become a 'city' failing in 2012.

The town's motto sums things up; it means Beauty and Health. *Aptly, Bournemouth was named Europe's prettiest town in 1995, winning the* Entente Florale Europe.

A Brief History

So, no history? When people say this, they're thinking of the resort that grew around the mouth of the Bourne stream. This 'Bourne mouth' was tiny at first, but grew rapidly, swallowing up much of the surrounding area and absorbing places of far greater antiquity, which now make up the modern borough of Bournemouth.

On Hengistbury Head, Stone Age flint implements and Bronze Age barrows have been found, and in the Iron Age there was a thriving port here. A Neolithic skull, 'the Bournemouth man', was unearthed in 1932 at Longham – actually a misnomer because Longham is outside Bournemouth borough and it was a woman's skull. Bronze Age barrows have been discovered in Moordown, Iford and Longbarrow Close near Cooper Dean, while Hillbrow Road in Pokesdown was the site of a Bronze Age cemetery. Iron Age remains have been discovered in Strouden, Kinson and, in 1969, on the East Cliff near the Carlton Hotel.

In the 12th century the region around the mouth of the Bourne was part of the Hundred of Holdenhurst. The area we know today as Bournemouth was originally a barren heathland, used as a hunting estate called Stourfield Chase in Tudor times. The first mention of 'Bournemouth' seems to have been in 1407 in the *Christchurch Priory Cartulary* (manuscripts/charters), when the washing up of a large fish was recorded, but this was a reference only to a geographical area (around the mouth of the Bourne stream). In 1574, the Earl of Southampton, worried about French or Spanish enemy landing, noted that the area was 'devoid of all habitation'. If only he could see it now. Apart from the hunting estate and a few fields, it was largely common land. There was a cottage called Decoy Pond House where sportsmen waited for game to arrive on the adjacent pond (originally sited at the beginning of today's Upper Gardens). This is later believed to be Bourne House, shown on Isaac Taylor's *Map of Hampshire* (1759), in today's Square. Early 17th-century maps reveal mining in the area, with 'copperas works' at Alum Chine and Boscombe, Bournemouth's first and short-lived flirt with industry.

In the 18th century, smugglers were active, making good use of the deserted coastline with its 'barren, uncultivated heath' (Duke of Rutland, 1805), along with local turf cutters and fishermen. The most famous smuggler in the Bournemouth area was Isaac Gulliver, who had been active elsewhere in Dorset before descending on Longham in the late 1770s, then Kinson in 1780, an ideal spot for concealing contraband because of the lack of nearby habitation. Kinson is said to have become a warren of secret tunnels, and the churchyard of St Andrew's on Millhams Road has smugglers' graves. Gulliver's exploits became legendary, including one occasion when he is alleged to have

Bournemouth's cliffs of gravel, sand and clay were laid down in the Tertiary era (around 65 million years ago).

faked his own death to thwart Revenue men. Gulliver might have remained an obscure figure but for his business acumen following receipt of a Royal pardon (1782), when he completed several land acquisitions around Kinson and West Moors. Henry Perlee Parker painted *Smugglers at Bourne Mouth*, which it is believed depicts 'Old Gulliver' as the central figure. The painting was once displayed in the Tregonwell Arms, a favourite smugglers' meeting place, which later became popular with visitors because of its tea gardens. It was demolished in the 1880s.

Modern Bournemouth begins not with Lewis Tregonwell but with Sir George Ivison Tapps, Lord of the Manor of Christchurch, who benefitted from the Christchurch Inclosure Act of 1802 and bought 205 acres of heath, which he proceeded to clear, plant with pines and develop. He built the Tapps Arms (later Tregonwell Arms) public house in 1809 where today's Post Office Road and Old Christchurch Road join, later selling this to Tregonwell along with land for a house in Exeter Road. Tregonwell proceeded to build holiday villas, the beginning of the seaside resort we know today.

The Tregonwell Arms. (Photographer S.G. Witcomb, Yeovil, April 1883. Courtesy of Bournemouth Libraries.)

Tregonwell's first house, originally named The Mansion (today the Royal Exeter Hotel on Exeter Road) was rapidly followed in 1810/11 by a second house built nearby for his butler Symes (thatched Symes Cottage, which became Tregonwell House, then Portman Lodge, after Mrs Tregonwell's maiden-name). It caught fire in 1922 and was demolished in 1930, the site later occupied by Hants and Dorset Bus Station.

Tregonwell and Tapps collaborated, planting Scots pines, and then the Maritime pines Bournemouth would become famous for, Tregonwell believing that 'pine-scented air' was beneficial for sufferers of lung conditions, especially tuberculosis. Today's Pine Walk in the Lower Gardens was originally called Invalids' Walk, and thus Bournemouth found its first calling as a 'resort' for those in poor health.

Invalids' Walk c 1903. (Source Wikimedia Commons.)

After Tapps' death, his son, Sir George William Tapps-Gervis, oversaw further development of Bournemouth, which he envisioned as rivalling Brighton and Weymouth. He employed local architect Benjamin Ferrey, who designed the town's first hotel, today's Royal Bath Hotel, which opened in 1838, with the Belle Vue boarding house following in 1841. He also bore the cost of creating St Peter's, the town's mother church. John Sydenham established a library and reading rooms in 1840 within the Belle Vue Hotel, which later moved to new premises near the pier. There was also a post office and booking office for the pleasure cruises that operated from the pier. (The building was finally replaced in 1937 by the Pier Approach Baths, offering a range of seawater treatments. Popular aqua shows were also held here until 1984.)

Bournemouth's future as a resort was a little way off: in 1851 it ranked 69th on Britain's 'resort list', its permanent population a mere 695. Early emphasis on health was evident with establishment of the Royal National Sanatorium (Royal National Chest Hospital, for consumption and diseases of the chest) in Bourne Avenue in 1855, the first purpose-built sanatorium, with chalets and shelters in the Gardens.

The Grove is a Victorian hotel that found a new purpose in June 2011, as a respite holiday retreat catering for cancer patients and those suffering with other terminal illnesses and their carers. It is owned by Macmillan Caring Locally, a charity formed in 1974 to support a palliative care unit at Christchurch Hospital, and is unique in the UK. Brenden Howard (recipient of a South West Tourism Gold Unsung Hero Award 2017) is the manager:

'Bournemouth was originally a health resort before becoming a fully-fledged holiday destination, so, in a sense, history is repeating itself here. We aim to make the Grove as much like a regular hotel as possible, but with the extra reassurance that there is a qualified nurse on call for any emergencies 24 hours a day. We have 30 rooms, all accessible by lift, including three with electric profiling beds and en-suite wet rooms that are always taken. We have many guests who return to us, sometimes many times over. Once a patient has been diagnosed and referred here by a GP or health professional, they are welcome to keep returning should they enter remission or be completely cured (one guest came here 26 times in 3–4 years!) We have the lovely gardens at the hotel that the guests can enjoy, but we also have a beach hut (with free passes for the East Cliff Lift) and a coach we use for trips out into the surrounding area. These are free of charge for our guests. As people of all ages come here at a difficult time in their lives, we aim to operate this just like a normal hotel with a friendly and welcoming ambience, which provides respite for the carers, amidst an air of normality. We get to know the guests, especially those who return, and they become like part of the family. We also provide that individual touch. Our chefs greet guests with special dietary requirements on arrival. We have a lovely characterful building here, but it is the great team of staff we have that really makes the place what it is.'

Outside the BIC is a statue of Creeke, sat on a toilet, which I like to think is a compliment!

The Bournemouth Improvement Act (1856) gave the modest watering place and health resort the power to become a town, and the architect and surveyor most responsible for that town's early shaping was Christopher Crabb Creeke. As well as contributing 'meandering roads and spacious villas', he rationalised the town's drainage, water supply and refuse collection. It was around the time Creeke arrived (c 1850) that Bournemouth also got its first permanent barber. Before that, someone travelled over from Christchurch twice a week. That's how little demand there had been! The town's first newspaper, the *Bournemouth Visitors' Directory*, appeared in June 1858.

The Lansdowne began emerging around 1863 and was almost certainly named after Lansdowne Crescent in Bath, another spa. Gas lighting arrived in 1864 and a town-crier a year later. Arcades sprang up for the benefit of shoppers. Henry Joy built Gervis Arcade (Bournemouth Arcade) between 1866 and 1873, then Westbourne Arcade in 1884. There was someone to take pictures of Bournemouth's development, as Robert Day became its first photographer. He had a studio-hut at the foot of Richmond Hill. Electricity was longer coming; an 'electric light exhibition' took place at Dean Park Cricket Ground in 1878, with the Bournemouth and District Electric Lighting Company formed in 1891.

Making that leap from convalescence to commercialism, Bournemouth began to provide for visitors, with a pier and other 'entertainments'. Today's 228-m (750-ft)-long pier was constructed between 1878 and 1880 by Eugenius Birch, following an earlier (1855/56) wooden 30-m (100-ft) jetty, slightly to the east, and a 304-m (1000-ft) wooden pier (1859–61) built by

Pier Approach c 1884. (Courtesy of Tim Phillips, National Piers Society.)

George Rennie. The pier provided easier facilities for berthing ships, the first regular passenger steamship to ply from Bournemouth Pier being the *Heather Bell* in 1871. One-seater donkey carriages conveyed invalids from the likes of Manor Road to the pier and town (with over a hundred such bath-chair proprietors in 1914), while travelling fairs entertained on the beach until 1907 when the Undercliff was built. The pier was extended in 1909, but lost its magnificent Victorian Gothic entrance in 1930.

Southbourne Pier, designed by Archibald Smith, opened in August 1888. It was located off the end of Warren Edge Path, built of iron, based on iron piles driven into the sand and clay, with a pier head and landing stage. Just 2 years later, the pier and sea walls built to protect it suffered extensive storm damage, and two more storms in 1900/01 finished it off. There being no spare money available for repairs, it was later demolished in 1909.

The former clock tower on the roof of the James Fisher Medical Centre, Tolpuddle Gardens, Muscliff, came from the old Bournemouth Pier entrance (demolished in 1930), and now has stained glass by the celebrated Dorset stained-glass artist Henry Haig.

Ill-fated Southbourne Pier. (Courtesy of Bournemouth Libraries.)

Boscombe Pier was also designed by Archibald Smith. Its first pile was driven home by Lady Jane Shelley (the wife of Percy Florence, son of Mary Shelley) in October 1888 and the pier opened in July 1889, at a cost of £12,000, with the Duke of Argyll presiding. The first vessel sailing from here was Sir Percy Shelley's own steam yacht *Oceana*. The 'Boscombe Whale' was a popular attraction for many years. After being washed up on the beach in January 1897, the 65-ft-long skeleton (supposedly a Blue Whale) was put on display on the pier, attracting visitors and tourists for the next 30 years.

The original wrought-iron Boscombe Pier was rebuilt using reinforced concrete in the 1950s. Its modernist look is due to additions by John Burton in the 1960s.

The pier was originally 600 ft long; then, in the 1920s the sea end was reconstructed, at which time the Quarter Deck Theatre opened, which had an unusual canvas roof that could be unfurled in fine weather. The Mermaid Theatre which replaced the Quarter Deck opened as a roller-skating rink in 1962 but closed in 1989 and was dismantled in 2007. The pier is 750 ft in length today.

Public services and buildings were also needed. Bournemouth's first policeman arrived in 1856, with a police station built in today's Madeira Road in 1869. The first town hall (1875) was in Town Hall Avenue (a plaque commemorates this in Old Christchurch Road where the Criterion Arcade used to be). The next town hall was in Albert Road (the Theatre Royal site, 1887), followed by Yelverton Road (1892). The final move was in 1921 to today's Town Hall on Bourne Avenue, the former Mont Dore Hotel. Bournemouth got its first polling station in 1865 (as part of 'Christchurch'). In 1918, Bournemouth elected its own MP for the first time (two MPs from 1948), and in 1919 its first female councillor, Florence Elizabeth Laney.

The town's first post office was installed in the Tregonwell Arms in 1839; after many interim moves, it settled in Post Office Road in 1896 (the site now occupied by Pizza Express), finally moving in 2011 round the corner into WH Smith. The first fire service in Bournemouth started in 1870, with the central station in Holdenhurst Road built in 1902, the last of the town's 'original' fire stations still standing (now used as a nightclub). More recently, an inshore lifeboat operated from a small boathouse beneath the pier between 1965 and 1972. Today, lifeboats based at Mudeford and Poole collaborate on searches and respond to local incidents.

To begin with, local denizens resisted the railway's coming, thinking it would spoil the ambience of their town, but it finally arrived in 1870, via an extension of the Ringwood to Christchurch railway. The first station (Bournemouth East) was built on the other side of Holdenhurst Road from today's Bournemouth train station. Bournemouth West off Queen's Road (today's Bourne Close) came into service in 1874, as the terminus for the Somerset and Dorset Joint Railway and for trains from London.

Bournemouth West Station. (Courtesy of Bournemouth Libraries.)

The rather basic Bournemouth East station was replaced by a more substantial Bournemouth Central station in 1885, across the road (in its present location). The station hosted a touching farewell in March 1898 when former Liberal Prime Minister William Ewart Gladstone caught a train home after recuperation. His impromptu speech on the platform is said to have been his final public appearance, as he died within 2 months. He ended with 'God bless you all, and this place, and the land we love'. Pokesdown station opened in 1886. By the turn of the 20th century there were another two stations: Boscombe and the long-forgotten Meyrick Park Halt (which closed in 1917). Plans for a more 'central' station near Braidley Road were never acted upon. The town's most famous train, the *Bournemouth Belle*, ran between 1931 and 1967. Bournemouth Central was renamed simply Bournemouth Station in 1967, following closure of Bournemouth West after electrification of the line from Waterloo to Bournemouth.

A special piece of Bournemouth transport history was the foundation of Royal Blue Coach Operators by Thomas Elliott in 1880, with horses stabled at mews in Norwich Avenue and a booking office on Richmond Hill. Starting

Bournemouth's growth accelerated with arrival of the railways, and today the town attracts over 5 million visitors annually.

with horse-drawn vehicles and stagecoaches and charabancs, Royal Blue purchased its first motor-driven charabanc in 1913 and its first coach service to London began in 1919. By 1930, the company was operating 11 routes, including to Birmingham and Bristol. The Elliott family sold the business in 1934 and it then became government-owned in 1947, but still retained its Royal Blue name, peaking in 1965, when it carried 1½ million passengers. Royal Blue finally became part of National Express in 1973.

Trams were introduced in 1902 and the complete system from Christchurch to Poole was completed in 1906, courtesy of the Bournemouth Corporation Tramways Act of 1903. Bournemouth's network was also the first in Britain to combine overhead and underground electrical conduit systems; the latter, installed in an effort to avoid unsightly overhead wiring, was abandoned in 1911 owing to technical complications and maintenance costs. A serious accident occurred in May 1908, when a tram derailed in Avenue Road, killing seven passengers. Tram numbers peaked at 131, plus a breakdown tram, yet they were relatively short-lived, as an experimental trolley-bus service began in 1933, which had completely taken over by 1936, with a maximum fleet of 104. The old tram lines still came in useful, reinforcing the concrete sea wall. All modes of transport have their fans; when the last trolley-buses ran in April 1969, people travelled from as far as Huddersfield for one final ride.

The *Bournemouth Daily Echo* (commonly known as the *Echo*) has been reporting news since 1900 and witnessed many changes affecting the town and its people. Poole native Darren Slade joined the newspaper towards the end of 1998, when the office had just one computer connected to the Internet, and is now Business and Technology Editor.

'We've covered some big stories from this office in the past, such as the controversial IMAX (which was going up around the time I started!) and the closure and demolition of the Winter Gardens. The human psyche is such that bad news does sell newspapers. We're conscious of balancing good and bad news though and there has been plenty of positive change to report recently, with money coming into the town in the shape of the new Hilton and the BH2 Odeon complex on the old bus station site. I'm sure this is a trend that is likely to continue, although that tension will still exist between making progress and preserving the heritage that we have. Whereas change has been slow to occur in the past, things do now seem to be happening apace. We don't just have the newspaper. Our online reporting is popular too, for example, with details of new restaurant openings, which get gobbled up (sorry!).

Bournemouth has become increasingly outward looking, with the two universities, Bournemouth and Arts University Bournemouth (AUB), and the tech businesses that have started up. I've observed first-hand the town becoming more cosmopolitan, with a younger demographic. I suspect that "Blue Rinse Bournemouth" has probably been consigned to the history books now, if it ever existed. The phenomenal rise of the Cherries to the Premiership has been good for the town and for the newspaper. We all remember the club's dark days too though: the periods in administration, when it looked as though the club might lose its League status, or even go under. The Air Show is another phenomenal success story, which also gives the paper a welcome sales "spike".

The Echo *still has a visible presence in Bournemouth, although the printing moved to Southampton in 1997 (and is now done in Weymouth). Our prestigious 1932 Art-Deco building has seen some recent changes. THAT Group has overseen the former print room's transformation into THIS Workspace, where short business rents can be taken out – ideal for start-up companies.*

I'm sure we'll see further changes for the rest of the building, which should guarantee the Echo's *long-term future in this, its spiritual home. I certainly appreciate being able to work in this inspiring iconic building, which is everything a newspaper building should be. It puts me in mind of Clark Kent and the* Daily Planet!'

Bournemouth beach can be accessed via a pleasant stroll from the town centre through the Lower Gardens to Pier Approach, which has been revamped several times over the years.

By 1860, Bournemouth had shed its image of being an invalids' watering-place and was firmly on its way to being a holiday resort rivalling the country's best. It held on to its genteel ambience, however, and attracted the well-to-do. One famous visitor was Guglielmo Marconi, who was staying at the seafront Madeira Hotel in June 1898 when he received the world's first paid radio message from Lord Kelvin on the Isle of Wight. Marconi fell out with the hotel management, shifting his equipment to a nearby house, Sandhills. Bournemouth played its part then in the development of long-distance radio transmission. It was a mantle later picked up by Harold Sydney Geneen, who was born in 1910 in Bournemouth but became a US-based director of Raytheon and later ITT. The BBC Wireless Studio at 72 Holdenhurst Road was Bournemouth's first local radio station in October 1923 (6BM Radio until June 1939) and used Marconi equipment. I guess the town has always been forward-thinking; it was one of the first to have a telephone.

In 1907 the first part of the Undercliff, from Bournemouth Pier to Meyrick Road, opened. Electrically operated lifts to connect the town and Undercliff soon followed, with East Cliff Lift and West Cliff Lift opening in 1908 (a third lift at Fisherman's Walk opened in 1935). Undercliff Drive developed in the early 20th century partly as an amenity and partly to reinforce the cliffs.

With boundary extensions Bournemouth was growing. The first extension in 1876 incorporated Boscombe and Springbourne, then in 1885 Westbourne, Meyrick Park and Malmesbury Park; 1901 saw Winton, Moordown, Richmond Park, Pokesdown and Southbourne included. The 1931 extension saw the town take Kinson from Poole. At the same time, Holdenhurst, the

'mother of Bournemouth', joined the bourgeoning 'new town'. For 10 days in July 1910 the town celebrated its first 100 years with lavish centenary fetes, which included an international aviation meeting at a specially laid-out grass aerodrome at Southbourne between Tuckton and Double Dykes near Hengistbury Head.

The town's gentility did not protect it from the exigencies of war, however. In 1907, German Kaiser Wilhelm II visited Bournemouth, his cavalcade driving through The Square. His popularity did not last though, and during WWI, Horatio Bottomley, editor of *John Bull* (magazine), presided over a mock-trial of the Kaiser in Bournemouth. After the war, large crowds greeted the arrival of the Admiral of the Fleet David Beatty and Field Marshal Douglas Haig, who were both awarded the Freedom of Bournemouth (the first recipient was Field Marshal Roberts in 1902).

When war-clouds gathered again, a Bournemouth-born diplomat, Sir Horace Wilson, delivered a personal letter from British PM Neville Chamberlain to Hitler in Berlin. It was all in vain though. Come WWII, residents and visitors saw machine guns atop Bournemouth's taller buildings (the Town Hall, Beales and Highcliff Hotel). Thousands of Allied troops, including at least 10,000 Canadians, were billeted in the town during the war, many in the requisitioned hotels.

The impact of war was hard felt with the air-raid of 23 May 1943, Bournemouth's worst day. On that quiet Sunday, 25 bombs were dropped, destroying 22 buildings and damaging over 3,000 more, nearly 40 of which had to be demolished. Numbers of deaths vary, but it is estimated between 130 and 208 people were killed, mostly Allied airmen billeted at the Metropole Hotel. A memorial was unveiled 70 years later at the Lansdowne, close to the site of the Metropole. This was the worst of 50-odd air-raids Bournemouth suffered, which saw over 2,200 bombs fall on the town during WWII, killing up to 350 civilians and servicemen, with nearly 14,000 buildings affected: 75 destroyed, 171 demolished as beyond repair, 675 badly damaged but repairable, over 9000 slightly damaged and over 3000 suffering broken glass. Redemption after the awful 1943 bombing would have been in mind when Field Marshal Montgomery, Dwight Eisenhower and other Allied commanders stayed at the Carlton Hotel on the East Cliff in May 1944 as they presided over D-Day rehearsals in Poole Bay. Both piers had gaps cut to stop them being used by the enemy. After the war, Donald Bailey OBE, inventor of the Bailey bridge, which Monty believed hastened the end of the war, spent his retirement in Bournemouth.

Despite its relative infancy, the town has received numerous royals over the years. Many of Queen Victoria's children visited. Eldest son Edward (later King Edward VII) first came to Bournemouth as a youngster with his tutor, staying at the Bath Hotel in 1856, hence its later name the Royal Bath. In 1877 Edward had the Red House built in Derby Road for the 'benefit' of his then-mistress, Lillie Langtry. Edward opened the Royal Victoria Hospital in Westbourne in 1890, the town's memorial to Victoria's Golden Jubilee. A west wing to the hospital was later opened by Victoria's third son, Prince Arthur, Duke of Connaught and Strathearn. He also performed the honours at Boscombe Arcade's opening in 1892. Princess Beatrice, Victoria's youngest child, was received by Lady Russell-Cotes at East Cliff Hall (the future museum) in 1902. She returned in February 1919 to open new galleries on the 59th anniversary of the Russell-Cotes' wedding. Future King Edward VIII visited in 1927, attending the Disabled Sailors' and Soldiers' Workshops, which were set up to provide work for 18 disabled ex-servicemen after WWI. He also opened Boscombe Promenade, east of the pier. Queen Elizabeth II and Prince Philip came to Bournemouth in 1966, the first visit by a reigning monarch, when she opened Kings Park Athletics Centre. They returned in March 1979 to view the computerised control room at Madeira Road police station. The Queen also visited in 1988 and 2004, when she opened an extension to the athletics stadium. Diana, Princess of Wales, opened the new headquarters of retirement-home developers McCarthy & Stone in Bournemouth in December 1987.

For much of the history described in this book I am indebted to previous historians, but also those still working to uncover Bournemouth's past. One such is Andrew Emery who also happens to be the council's Resort Development and Strategic Planning Manager. I found it reassuring that all tourism-related planning applications are referred to Andrew, who is also the author of *A History of Bournemouth Seafront* (2008).

'Writing the book ran nicely alongside our future planning for Bournemouth seafront where we have a 20-year vision that balances progress with preservation. It's very important when considering future development not to lose sight of the history, of where we've come from, and the things that make this resort unique. I like to think that appreciation of history informs our thinking, helping us to get decisions right. I was involved in the Boscombe Overstrand regeneration where we were delighted to involve Wayne Hemingway in a project that has revitalised that part of the seafront. Bournemouth is not an "identikit" town and we need to stay true to the reasons why people have wanted to come here, whilst also keeping the resort going. We have a real responsibility to get things right so that future generations can continue to enjoy what we have. The council has retained control of its coastal strip, so is in a unique position to guide and influence the development of this going forward.

My real passion, historically, is the seafront and the Lower Gardens. I've led guided walks where I've dressed up as one of our Victorian forefathers, for example, the architects Eugenius Birch and Decimus Burton, or author Robert Louis Stevenson, all of whom have links with Bournemouth. Talking of Stevenson, we'd certainly like to do more with the site of his Westbourne home "Skerryvore", possibly with a new trail from the beach, with steps leading up to the house from Alum Chine. I believe there is still much to be discovered about Bournemouth's history, for example, with its smuggling past, where I feel we've only started to scratch the surface.'

Boscombe Overstrand.

Rivers and Seafront

When modern Bournemouth emerged in the early 19th century, it was laid out around the mouth of the River Bourne (hence the name 'Bournemouth'). The Bourne is formed from the confluence of two springs – one at Knighton Bottom, the other at Bourne Bottom on Canford Heath. The Bourne flows from Coy Pond Gardens, just inside the borough of Poole, through Bournemouth's Upper Gardens and Central Gardens, disappearing under The Square, to pop up again meandering through the Lower Gardens, disappearing once more before flowing out to sea just east of the Pier.

Upper Gardens.

Lower Gardens.

The River Stour forms the boundary of the borough in places. Stour Valley Nature Reserve and Kingfisher Barn Visitor Centre are in Muscliff, and riverside walks can be enjoyed in either direction, west towards Ensbury or east towards Throop (see Walk 7). A good place to access the river is from Granby Road car park off Muscliffe Lane. At Throop it is possible to cross the mill stream at the sluices and then cross the river bridge above the weir, heading towards Hurn and the airport. The Stour continues north of Holdenhurst village and is joined by the Moors River, before going under the A338 Spur Road, the river forming a boundary between Bournemouth and Christchurch as it heads south and east towards Christchurch Harbour.

Sluice gates and mill pond at Throop Mill.

River Stour at Tuckton Bridge.

Bournemouth is principally attractive for its 7 miles of award-winning beaches, pleasant climate and lovely Poole Bay, with views of the Isle of Wight and Purbeck Hills. Combined with Poole's four Blue Flags, the bay has been awarded more Blue Flags than any other beach area in the UK. Beaches at Alum Chine, Middle Chine, Fisherman's Walk and Hengistbury Head are dog-friendly between 1 May and 30 September.

The sweep of the bay from Hengistbury Head towards Bournemouth.

Hengistbury Head beach.

Hengistbury Head (also known as Solent beach) has a quiet, natural beach, a mix of sand and shingle, popular with sea fishermen, kite flyers and picnickers. There are six other named beaches – Alum Chine, Durley Chine, Fisherman's Walk, Southbourne, Bournemouth and Boscombe – together with four attractive chines (valleys) – Boscombe, Alum, Middle and Durley (Branksome Dene Chine is just over the border in Poole). The word 'chine' is peculiar to Dorset and the Isle of Wight and has several derivatives: from the Saxon *cinan* meaning gap and Old English *cinu* meaning a fissure or narrow valley. The chines are principally works of nature, and make the seafront different here to most other British resorts.

Boscombe Chine (or Gardens) is the most easterly chine and can be entered off the roundabout facing Boscombe Pier. When the pier was officially re-opened by Mayor J.E. Beale in 1904 (the council having purchased it the previous year), the pier and gardens were lit with 18,000 fairy lamps. Towards the foot of the chine near Sea Road was discovered a chalybeate (ferruginous) spring, the waters of which were imbibed for their health-giving mineral content and also bottled and sold as aerated table water. Sir Henry Drummond Wolff (1830–1908) erected a small thatched building around the spring, which attracted visitors.

Boscombe Chine Gardens.

Alum Chine is the longest of Bournemouth's chines, home to the beautiful Tropical Gardens. The beach here has received both Green and Blue Flag awards, and there is parking at the foot of Alumhurst Road. The name comes from Allom House and the 6th Lord Mountjoy's attempts to work alum (a tanning preservative and dyeing fixative) and copperas (a dye/ink fixative) in this area from 1564. He is credited as the first English manufacturer of alum, which was also used by illuminators and painters and in medicine by all accounts. The mining proved uneconomic and had ceased by the mid-17th century. Alum Chine, previously heathland, changed during the late 19th and early 20th centuries, when the present mix of evergreen and deciduous woodland was planted.

Towards the top end of Alum Chine.

The chine is crossed by three bridges dating to 1903, 1922 and 1924. Young Winston Churchill had a narrow escape in January 1893 (aged 18) when he leapt from an earlier rustic bridge into a fir tree, falling nearly 30 ft to the ground, rendering himself unconscious for 3 days and bed-bound for 3 months with a ruptured kidney. It was allegedly during this period of inactivity that he developed his interest in politics. He was staying at the time with Lord and Lady Wimborne at their home Branksome Dene (it has also been claimed the rustic bridge may have been in Branksome Dene Chine itself. If so, it certainly doesn't exist today). Churchill revisited the area in July 1940 when inspecting sea defences being constructed to face the threat of German invasion. Among the obstacles were pipe-mines at the base of the chines.

Rhododendron-bordered West Overcliff Drive snakes around the east side of Alum Chine, then around both sides of Middle Chine, which it crosses via a bridge, before heading up the west side of Durley Chine. An overflow channel drops down the side of Middle Chine from West Overcliff Drive with a sign 'Warning floodwater spillway no thoroughfare'. Middle Chine is one of the smaller, shorter chines, with a gentle descent to the sea, and is located about halfway between Alum Chine and Durley Chine. The trees would have been fairly newly planted in Victorian times, so there is considerably more shade today than then. About half-way down is the impressive West Overcliff Drive road bridge, with a set of steps up. The sea is glimpsed through the trees, before the view opens up as you approach the bottom of the chine.

Durley Chine once formed the boundary between Hampshire and Dorset: by 1818 this had moved a little further west to County Gates. The name is thought to have been 'borrowed' from Durley (a village near Bishop's Waltham, Hants, owned by the Cooper-Dean family), and it certainly featured on a local map of 1805. The chine is a pleasant, shady amble between pine-clad banks, the stream hidden away in a pipe below the road. White pipe-clay was found here (also east of Boscombe), which was worked out and sent to the Staffordshire potteries for the making of porcelain. The chine was also known as Big Durley Chine in the past to distinguish it from Little Durley Chine. Early guidebooks also talk of Water Chine, a small inlet close to West Cliff Lift. Joseph's Steps once led down the cliff between Little Durley Chine and the site of today's West Cliff Lift. These were built by Joseph Cutler using timber from the wrecked pier of 1861, but were replaced by today's West Cliff Zig-Zag in the late-1930s. Also, a carriage once used to convey passengers from the shoreline, up the chine, to West Cliff Road. Today there is parking, toilets and cafés at the beach.

The pier has seen many changes. In fact, the landing stages either side (replaced with new timber) are the only original design feature remaining from Birch's 1880 pier. Some of its past entertainments seem quite passé now, for example, deck games such as giant chess and draughts, deck quoits and shuffle-board. The pier was established not only for promenading, but also as a jetty for steamship pleasure cruisers. After regular sailings began in 1871, vessels provided trips around the bay and further afield to the likes of Poole, Swanage, Lulworth, Weymouth, the Isle of Wight, Portsmouth, Brighton, Torquay, and even the Channel Islands and Cherbourg. There was once a separate landing platform just east of the pier, used by pleasure boats offering trips around the bay; this certainly existed in the 1950s, but there is no trace of it now. Briefly, after WWI, there was a 'water aerodrome' south of the Pier. Summer flying boat services to Southampton and the Isle of Wight were operated by Supermarine Aviation.

Pier Approach, with its seafront attractions, restaurants and cafés, and great views of the bay.

Boscombe beach has been transformed via the Boscombe Spa Village redevelopment scheme and is now home to various activities either side of the pier. The Overstrand here was National Coastal Regeneration Project of the Year at the National Regeneration Awards 2010. Wayne Hemingway MBE and Gerardine Hemingway MBE are cofounders of the 'Red or Dead' fashion label. As 'HemingwayDesign' they are urban and interior designers who are passionate about regeneration.

'Everything we do is creative and brave, as we don't want to repeat what has been done before. Boscombe, as a place, has had its problems, but we could see that the surf reef would galvanise the media. The surf reef has had some big hiccups, but it's a bold, innovative move. It got people talking. When we saw the modernist Boscombe Overstrand, a building that had lain empty for 17 years, which some thought should be pulled down, we could see the potential for a watersports-based location, with a cool café, and it has worked well in terms of bringing the upper levels back into well-designed and well-appointed "surf pods". We like to maintain contact and keep tabs on our projects, so it has been gratifying to return and see the café doing well and the once-deserted beach now well frequented. I would say this has become the coolest part of Bournemouth beach and it's playing its part in lifting the perception of Boscombe as a place. The beautiful restoration of the pier has been important too, and the surf reef, derided by some, has helped. Without that courageous step, the rest wouldn't have followed. This end of Bournemouth is going only one way now, and that is up.'

Sand dunes occur along the clifftop of Boscombe and Southbourne beaches, some reaching a height of 40 ft, with marram grass binding them together. The shore is perfect for bathing and paddling. Due to the Isle of Wight, Bournemouth unusually has a double-tide – the main Channel tide,

coming from the west; then a few hours later, a subsidiary tide, which leaves the main tide beyond the island, working its way back via the Solent to Bournemouth. It's about a 20-minute promenade from Boscombe to the Blue Flag award-winning beach at Fisherman's Walk, Southbourne.

Fisherman's Walk beach and zig-zag.

Several seafront offices are located along the 7 miles, with dedicated teams providing information. Seafront Rangers offer advice on enjoying the seafront, while *LV=KidZone* is a child-safety scheme which issues wristbands to children in July and August (different colours for different zones); specially trained staff can then help reunite missing children with their families. In 2018, the team distributed 72,400 wristbands and helped 192 children and families.

Bournemouth is one of the UK's safest beaches, with RNLI lifeguards based all along the bay throughout the season.

For ease of access to the beach there are three cliff lifts – at West Cliff, East Cliff (currently closed) and Fisherman's Walk. These operate from the beginning of April (or earlier depending on when Easter falls) to end of October. Jeremy Foy is a seasonal member of staff currently based at the West Cliff.

'I work the top lift. We're open from 10:00 to 17:30, extending to 18:15 in the school summer holidays. The lifts run on demand, rather than to a timetable, so we'll always check to see if anyone else is coming before we set them off, although no-one would have to wait very long. The two operators can communicate via a visual check, buzzer or phone. I began on the East Cliff Lift in 1992 (until 2000) and came back in 2008. After the 2016 cliff fall put the East Cliff Lift out of operation, I moved across to the West Cliff. The main perk of this job is the panoramic view. I can virtually see the whole of the 7 miles of beach from up here, so wouldn't swap it with any other job. ... The lift moves at about a half a metre per second, so it's about a 90-second journey overall. It's slow and sedate; Bournemouth's founding fathers would have approved!

The lift is 145 ft (44 m) long, has a gradient of 70.4% and track gauge of 5 ft 6 in (1,676 mm).

The lifts work on an automatic electrical operation and it's just the doors that are manually operated, so we mainly have to keep an eye on things. There are weekly checks by engineers and electricians to ensure that this 1908 technology is ticking along ok, and the lifts are extremely reliable and well maintained. Full marks to the Edwardian engineers! We've had some famous people in the lifts: the Cherries team that won the Football League Championship in 2015, World Cup winner Martin Peters, England manager Roy Hodgson (who only ventured into the toll house), Paul Weller the musician, Robert Lindsay the actor, and Evan Davis off Newsnight. Michael Portillo used the East Cliff Lift when he was here on one of his Great British Railway Journeys, *and, of course, because of the conferences, we've had lots of politicians going up and down!'*

There are also zig-zag pathways at various points along the cliff. East Cliff Zig-Zag, which replaced Meyrick Steps, was constructed in the winter of 1908/9 and cost the council £300. Retaining walls are of Purbeck stone, with recess benches, and bamboo has been planted in an attempt to stabilise the cliff face. The eight-sectioned descent is 38 m long. West Cliff Zig-Zag opened in the late-1930s and was re-opened in 1985 following major engineering work on the cliff. Manor Steps Zig-Zag is accessed from Boscombe Overcliff Drive, and Beacon Steps Zig-Zag links Beacon Road to the promenade (West Cliff).

Bathing machines are first mentioned in Bournemouth in 1826 and by 1831 there were at least three for hire. The man responsible for their introduction here was Samuel Bayly. By 1874 we were 'amply provided for by a goodly number of bathing machines', located between West Cliff and East Cliff Zig-Zags. The last of the old machines was broken up by 1930, replaced by hygienic 'bathing stations'. West of the pier is Happylands Arcade, which was originally a 1930s bathing station, with ground-floor shelters for deckchairs, segregated changing areas on the upper floor, and a roof sun terrace.

The next innovation was the beach hut. Approximately 10% of all beach huts in the UK are on Bournemouth seafront, with over 250 available for weekly hire. In fact, the first hut in the UK was erected here in 1909. Today, around 70% of Bournemouth's huts are privately owned. Hut 2359, close to Bournemouth Beach Office, is the oldest and has a blue plaque on its apex.

Sand sculptures are rarely seen here today, but one particularly talented exponent was John Suchomlin, who visited Bournemouth several times in the 1930s. His sculpture *'The Flight into Egypt'* (1935), which showed Mary, Joseph and the baby Jesus, was made on Bournemouth beach using only sand, water and colour. There used to be a sand sculpture display hut on the beach next to the pier.

The first beach hut.

Gardens and Nature Areas

Bournemouth's parks and gardens today are the legacy of the founding fathers who envisioned, first, a relaxing environment for those recuperating from illness, and second, a pleasant vista and amenity that would attract visitors and holidaymakers. There are around 2,000 acres of parks, gardens and open spaces within the borough, and ten sites are officially designated nature reserves (NR).

Bournemouth and District Horticultural Society was formed in 1884 and is one of the oldest organisations in the town. It was renamed Bournemouth Gardening Club in 2014. The club meets on the first Friday of each month at St Francis of Assisi Church Hall in Charminster.

A 'Bournemouth in Bloom' competition is judged each July, with a presentation in October. Staged annually, it has been running for over 30 years.

Gardens

Bournemouth's first gardens were the Westover Pleasure Gardens (once Westover Shrubberies), laid out over 1848/49 on the south-facing slope of Westover Road. Invalids' Walk here in the Lower Gardens followed in 1858 (renamed Pine Walk after WWI). The valley below Westover Gardens, known today as the Lower Gardens, remained rough, marshy grassland until attempts began from 1869 to beautify this as well.

Pine Walk in the Lower Gardens.

Pine trees are a characteristic of Bournemouth, abundant in many places, for example, Meyrick and Queens Parks, the Gardens and Horseshoe Common. The maritime pine (tall with large cones) was planted in such quantity that it became known as the 'Bournemouth pine'; look out too for Scots pine (with bright golden bark and its trademark scent), black pine (or Austrian pine), Monterey pine, white pine and Oregon pitch pine. The poet Rupert Brooke described Bournemouth as being full of 'moaning pines'. A specialist Arboricultural Team manages all the trees in Bournemouth, together with a band of volunteer Tree Wardens, run independently from, but supported by the council.

Bournemouth Gardens (c 29 acres) consist of the Lower, Central and Upper Gardens, extending for a total of 3 km from Bournemouth Pier to the boundary with Poole. All have been Green Flag winners since 1999 and are Grade II Listed in the English Heritage Register of Parks and Gardens. The town has always been proud of its gardens and floral displays and was Britain in Bloom winner in 1992, 1994 and 1995.

The Lower Gardens are quite short, running from the pier to The Square. The Pavilion rock garden was laid out in the late 1920s, the largest municipal rockery in the country at the time. It has been restored by the Lower Gardens Volunteer Group. Year-round attractions in the Gardens include mini-golf, the bandstand and aviary. Between May and September there is an open-air Art and Makers Market in Pine Walk. The summer months also see the Kids Free Fun Festival and traditional candlelight illuminations, while in winter an open-air ice rink appears. *Street Food Corner* food traders are close to the flyover by the

The rock garden below the Pavilion in the Lower Gardens.

Hermitage Hotel, together with other refreshment kiosks. This is the only section of the Gardens with public toilets.

The Central Gardens run north of The Square as far as the tennis courts and are formally planted. The cenotaph is located opposite the town hall, before you reach the tennis courts and café. There is also a play park, including a zip-wire.

The pergola adorning the bridge near The Square was installed in 1990 to mark the borough's centenary. It was created by re-using a cast-iron veranda from Boscombe rescued at the time the Sovereign Centre was being built.

The Upper Gardens are more natural, with a range of grasses and exotic trees such as Himalayan Cedar, Monkey Puzzle and Silver Fir. Extensive planting was undertaken in 1874, with refurbishment in 1992. Several small red wooden bridges cross the Bourne here. The Gothic-style water tower just downstream of Prince of Wales Road bridge was built in 1885 and used to house a

header tank, fed by a waterwheel pump. Water was used to irrigate flower beds and power an ornamental fountain. The wheel was removed during the war and the fountain no longer exists. The Upper Gardens continue to ornamental rockeries, blending into Coy Pond Gardens as you enter Branksome (Poole).

The beautiful floral displays around Bournemouth do not happen accidentally. Kings Park Nursery has been growing plants for the borough's parks and gardens since 1924. Nursery manager Chris Evans, a navy Falklands veteran, former computer programmer and one-time art student, is passionate about garden design.

Until 1851 the Upper Gardens were known as Decoy Pond Meadow. The water tower is now home to bats.

'We're very proud of the awards we've won: Britain in Bloom; Europe in Bloom; gold medals at Tatton; Gold at Chelsea, plus the President's Award, which I believe was unprecedented for a first time in show; Silver Gilt at Hampton Court; and winners of lots of regional competitions. I love trying to come up with something very different, for example, a "Light and Dark" display for Tatton (a show winner), which contrasted the town's tradition as a health resort with its Shelley Gothic horror side.

At Kings Park we aim to be green (of course), with our own biomass boiler, which burns wood that comes down in the park. I also want us to be emotive. We have a social services project, growing food that helps to supplement local schoolchildren's diets, and we have lots of volunteers, some of whom will be recovering, for example, from illness, or some other setback in their life. I only have 3.5 full-time staff here, so we do rely heavily on volunteers. Our other "volunteer" is the nursery cat, Fluffy, who takes precedence. We all work around her! We also want to try and make the nursery pay, so we have a public sale area, also growing for customers, including Christchurch and Poole.

The period from April to June is our busiest, when I'll be working 6–7 days each week. One of our main problems is time. The year goes so quickly, and we always seem to be running just behind, as well as preparing for the next season, when we know we'll have 1500 hanging baskets to get out, 70–80 pedestals and the bedding displays, which will be admired by some three million people in the Lower Gardens (that's a lot of critics if you get things wrong!). We face some of the same issues though as domestic gardeners. We have no control over the weather or seeds not germinating. Over the last 5 years we'll have used around 750 different types/species of plant and it's that kind of diversity, aided by the climate down here, which gives us the opportunity to grow unusual plants that makes it so interesting. I must be honest though. Although I've been involved in gardening since about 1990, I'm still learning!'

Historic Parks

Bournemouth's commoners had rights of 'turbary' (cutting turf for fuel) on five plots of land, rights they had virtually ceased to exercise by the early 1880s. Bournemouth Park Lands Act (1889) authorised using the plots as 'open spaces for the recreation and enjoyment of the public'. Frederick Lacey, a borough engineer and surveyor, was instrumental in the disposal of these plots.

Of Bournemouth's five large parks, Meyrick Park (194 acres), which opened in 1894, is closest to the town centre. The land and four other parks were given to Bournemouth by Sir George Meyrick. 'Father Christmas' (Cyril Beale) landed here in an aeroplane in 1912. A 'loop the loop' record (21 loops) was set over the park in 1914 by pioneering British aviator Gustav Hamel. It was also the venue for the annual display of Bournemouth Volunteer Fire Brigade. Meyrick Park water tower (built in 1900, and demolished in 1989) was the first ferro-concrete water tower in Britain. The park is home to a variety of sports, including golf which occupies half the acreage. Just west of the golf course, across Glenferness Avenue, is Pug's Hole, a small nature reserve and hidden gem, named after local smuggler 'Captain Pug' who is believed to have buried treasure here. Hidden away in the woods around Talbot Heath School, it consists of a valley with steep wooded slopes. Common birds seen here include woodpecker, nuthatch, coal tit and treecreeper.

Oakmeadians Rugby Club, Meyrick Park.

Kings Park (86½ acres) opened in 1902 to mark the coronation of King Edward VII. Common lizards and slowworms can be seen on the heath in summer. A small octagonal bandstand was removed from the end of Boscombe Pier and re-erected in Kings Park in 1906. There were once lion enclosures in the park, with the animals taken to the theatre in Boscombe, where they appeared in an indoor circus. Kings Park is known for its play areas, football and cricket; it also has a meadow and heathland conservation area to the north-west, with a small wooded area.

Queens Park (173 acres) also opened in 1902. With views of the New Forest, this park in the heart of Charminster includes a playground and café. The park is cared for in partnership with Queens Park Improvement and Protection Society (QUIPS). The area was originally known as Poors Common due to its poor-quality soil. Queens Park like Kings Park dates to 1902 and honours Edward VII's wife Alexandra. Queens Park's golf course (1905) is surrounded by one of the largest open areas in Bournemouth, which includes a large pond, home to water birds, damselflies and dragonflies.

Queens Park.

Other Public Open Spaces and Nature Reserves

Central Bournemouth and the West Cliff

Horseshoe Common (14 acres) connects Old Christchurch Road with Dean Park Road, with the A338 Wessex Way flying over the top. Blind Man's Pond was originally a sensory area for the blind, and is still valuable today for

Horseshoe Common.

wildlife. At one time, a stream ran from the pond down a steep ravine to join the Bourne, passing Plummers (Dingles) department store. Henry Joy was chastised for doing away with a well-known bridge crossing the stream when he built Gervis Arcade.

Wimborne Road Cemetery at the junction of Charminster and Wimborne Roads is Bournemouth's main cemetery. Known as Cemetery Junction, this was once Rush Corner (presumably not because people were rushing to get in here). It 'opened' in 1878 and is notable for its fine avenue of *Araucaria* (monkey puzzle) trees.

Argyll Gardens were originally planted in 1903, including a bowling green and croquet lawn, replaced by a pavilion and tennis courts in 1931, which in turn made way for a new pavilion and second bowling green in 1980.

Alum Chine's Tropical Gardens on West Overcliff Drive were laid out in the 1920s, in an area once used by local fishermen to store boats and equipment. They were replanted in 1996, with a paved viewing area. Dry-stone walls made of Portland stone form wave-like patterns evocative of the sea and its fishermen.

Alum Chime's Tropical Gardens.

Boscombe and Southbourne

The clifftop and nature reserve along Boscombe and Southbourne front includes exposed sandstone that is some 45 million years old and which supports over 300 plant species, making it a very rich botanical site for fauna and flora, with quirky names including suffocated clover and hairy bird's-foot trefoil. Insects include the grey bush-cricket, long-winged conehead and fly *Cephalops chlorinae*, which has only been recorded at one other site in Britain. The area is important for the nationally rare sand lizard (home to some 600 of them), wall and green lizards. The grassy scrub is also home to other rare species of flora and fauna, including the Dartford warbler, stonechat, greenfinch and kestrel. Look out for the 'beewolf' (predatory wasp), which hunts bees, carrying them off to its underground lair. More attractive are the butterflies (common blue, clouded yellow and painted lady).

It is difficult to imagine that Boscombe Cliff Gardens was once an industrial landscape, with men employed in brick fields. This 6-acre site merges into the Overcliff Nature Reserve and was opened in 1900. It overlooks the pier and the land train serves it sometimes. 'The Friends' help look after the gardens and organise events here. The Italianate garden was laid out on land given

by the Shelleys who gave Shelley Park and land stretching down to the shore. Apparently the columns in the garden came from the old swimming pool by the pier. The angled chalet house at the west end of the Italianate garden was Lady Shelley's seaside cottage where she could listen to the waves and watch for their yacht coming to the pier.

Italianate garden in Boscombe Cliff Gardens.

Boscombe Chine Gardens and Nature Reserve comprise a 9-acre site, with a water-themed playground. The Friends have produced a Tree Trail Leaflet (which can be downloaded – http://www.boscombechinegardens.org/).

Boscombe Chine Gardens.

Squirrel Café and minigolf in Boscombe Chine Gardens are council-owned, so by using them you are supporting the borough's local parks and open spaces. Knyveton Gardens is a lively pocket park of 4 acres in the middle of Boscombe and includes a bowls club and café.

In Southbourne, Fisherman's Walk has woodland, formal and informal planting, a bandstand, and an ornamental pond at the southern end. The name comes from the narrow path used by local fishermen from the 18th century who walked to their boats on the beach, this being a good place for mackerel fishing. After a long haul up the cliffs with their catch, the men headed to the New Bell Inn, founded in the late 1850s (today's Bell Inn opposite Pokesdown station). This was the nearest pub then! Fisherman's Walk was also used by smugglers. Today's ¼ mile 'Walk' is the boundary between Boscombe (west) and Southbourne (east) and was preserved as a park in 1913. Seafield Gardens on Tuckton Road is a recreation and sporting ground with a bowling club and tennis courts. The Grade II Listed water tower was built in 1875 to supply the 'Southbourne-on-Sea' area.

The 'Rest Gardens' at the far end of Fisherman's Walk, including the sunken pond, were officially opened in June 1937.

North Bournemouth

Turbary Common comprising 89 acres, the largest heathland area in north Bournemouth and an SSSI, is one of the borough's most important nature reserves. Rare and important species live here, including the Dartford warbler, all six species of British reptile and long-winged conehead crickets. Plants include the carnivorous sundew and bog asphodel. Grazing animals help manage the site.

Strouden Woods on Bradpole Road has some of Bournemouth's largest woodland areas. There are lots of birds, including Britain's smallest, the goldcrest. Moore Avenue in West Howe is a park and community area, which includes a community centre. Redhill Park runs alongside Redhill Avenue and has a playground, café and pitches. Redhill Common is a small (17¼ acres, reduced from 45) relic heathland site (now a nature reserve), lying just off the A3049 Wallisdown Road. The habitat here supports birds, reptiles and larger mammals, such as badgers and foxes. Redhill Common Conservation Group helps take care of the site.

Winton Recreation Ground (14 acres) is a green space in the busy area of Winton. This is a popular area for birds, and natural mulch in the flowerbeds provides a home for insects. Winton Rec was opened in 1906. Fampoux Gardens in Winton was renamed (from Green Road Pleasure Grounds) in 1923 to commemorate the action at Fampoux on 28 March 1918 which was part of the Battle of Arras, and in which the Hampshire Regiment played a prominent part. The gardens were relaid and a memorial built by some of the survivors of the battle to remember fallen comrades.

Kinson Common is a superb nature reserve hidden among Kinson's housing. Grazing animals help manage the site, which consists of woodland, SSSI heathland, marsh and meadow. Friends of Kinson Common help care for the site. Pelhams Park, in the heart of Kinson, just off Millhams Road, is looked after by Kinson Community Association and the Bowling Club Trust. The first building at Pelhams was built c 1788 on land owned by smuggler Isaac Gulliver. From the early 20th century the house and gardens were used more by the local community, before being sold to the council in 1930 for this express purpose. The park occupies around 8½ acres.

Grade II Listed Kinson Community Centre dates back to 1788, when the house was owned by Isaac Gulliver.

Millhams Mead, just north of Kinson and adjacent to the River Stour, began as a local tip in the 1960s and 1970s but has been transformed into a nature reserve of grassland, scrub and mature woodland. There are around 200 species of flowering plant, 24 species of butterfly and almost 50 species of bird. A self-guided walk called Gulliver's Trail leads you around the area (leaflets are available at the Kingfisher Centre).

Stour Valley Nature Reserve includes a 2-mile stretch of riverside path, meadow, hedgerow and woodland. Grazing animals help manage the habitat. Nearby, Muscliff Arboretum was established in 1983 and has an interesting selection of trees from around the world, with over 60 identification labels.

Muscliff Arboretum.

Littledown, Iford and Tuckton

Littledown Park, awarded a Green Flag Award in 2019, lies next to Littledown Centre and is a mix of calm oasis and leisure activity. Littledown Common runs from Kings Park and finishes behind the sports centre, with playgrounds at either end. Sheepwash, just east of Tesco (Castle Lane East), consists of

Tuckton Tea Gardens offer several amenities.

small wooded areas and meadow alongside the Stour, with a cycle path crossing the area. Along the river you may spot heron, egret, kingfisher and even otter. Iford Meadows, next to the Stour, has 150 different types of flowering plant. Grazing animals were introduced in 2011 to help manage the site and are usually grazing from September to April. Tuckton Tea Gardens and Riverlands off Wick Lane consist of a a large open space facing the Stour. The meadowland has lovely wildflowers.

Hengistbury Head/Solent Meads and Wick Fields

Home to over 500 plant species and 300 types of birds, Hengistbury Head/ Solent Meads and Wick Fields comprise one of the area's most important nature reserves. The Head is also a Stone Age, Bronze Age and Iron Age archaeological site. The Visitor Centre is open every day except Christmas Day and admission is free, although donations are welcome. It includes exhibition space, a shop and wildlife garden, and intimate webcams reveal what some wildlife is up to. The centre has up to six volunteers working each day, plus others helping with special events and maintaining the garden. Richard Hesketh is the Volunteer Coordinator.

'My responsibilities include putting together the centre's programme of events and walks, some of which I conduct myself. Bird walks are always popular, especially in the spring with all the bird-song. Astronomy walks also go down well, with the sky to the south being so clear. We undertake a lot of active management of the Head: for example, fencing off the Double Dykes and grazing Shetland sheep there achieves the double benefit of helping to preserve an ancient monument and enabling its shape to be better discerned. We also have Shetland cattle and Galloways performing the same function. Their grazing of Barn Field in winter benefits both the skylarks, who like the shorter grass at the start of the season, and the wildflowers, which have really come back. Laying down the hard-surfaced paths has also been beneficial, by reducing the erosion of some of the more sensitive habitats.

Wick Fields, part of Hengistbury Head Nature Reserve.

We've had nothing but positive comments about the visitor centre from the many thousands who've been here since it first opened. It's enhancing the visitors' experience, partly through informing them about why the Head is so special and why we need to look after it. We're trying to catch them early too with the likes of Toddlers' Tales, Pushchair Safaris and Wild Wednesdays, which can feature bug hunts, pond dipping and making birdhouses. We'd like to continue to evolve the offering and we want to get more people to know we're here. Having said that, we have had our famous visitors, including Sir Tom Courtenay and his wife!'

Hengistbury Head Visitor Centre is partly based in an old thatched barn, shown on Isaac Taylor's Map of Hampshire (1759) *as a 'summer house'.*

The Arts

A History of Art and Artists in the Area

Artists through the centuries have been inspired by Bournemouth, including William G. Hooper, Arthur Bell, Henry Perlee Parker (who painted *Smugglers at Bourne Mouth*), John Singer Sargent and William Strang (who produced portraits of R.L Stevenson), William Greenwood and Helen Constance Pym Sutton.

Bournemouth-born Lucy Kemp-Welch attended Bournemouth School of Art and was a talented equine artist who illustrated a 1915 edition of *Black Beauty*. She also produced WWI recruitment posters. In 1922 she was commissioned to paint two miniatures for Queen Mary's Dolls House (a gift from the nation to George V's queen, now in Windsor Castle).

Aubrey Beardsley (1872–98), a black-ink illustrator and author, came to Bournemouth hoping to be cured of TB, staying at Pier View, Boscombe, in 1896 and later Muriel, a corner-house in Terrace Road. While walking in Boscombe Chine, Beardsley suffered a haemorrhage, barely making it back to his hotel. He left Bournemouth in 1897, dying in France of TB the following year.

Commemorating the artist in Terrace Road is a plaque and mosaic representing a Beardsley design.

Boscombe-born Eustace Nash (1887–1969) was one of Bournemouth's most talented and influential artists. He sketched characters on the beach each week for the *Bournemouth Graphic* and his cartoons lampooned the Germans during WWI. He exhibited regularly at the Royal Academy. Leslie

Moffat Ward (1888–1978), a well-known local artist and engraver, was born in Worcester but lived and worked in Bournemouth most of his life. He taught at Bournemouth's Drummond Road Art School and Southern College of Art and lived at 22 Grants Avenue, Springbourne.

Paul Nash (1889–1946), the famous surrealist painter, war artist and photographer, had not long completed a watercolour of the view from his clifftop hotel bedroom (including a shelter above Honeycombe Chine) when he died in Boscombe. Frederick R. Fitzgerald (1897–1938), a painter of coastal and marine subjects, painted a view of the East Cliff before it developed, although it does feature East Cliff Lift. The picture can be seen in the Russell-Cotes.

The Art Scene Today

The open-air art exhibition in Pine Walk from May to September is one of the longest-running in the country, featuring the work of many local artists. There is also the Bournemouth and Poole Selfie Wall Trail. Conceived by Iain Alexander, seven artists have decorated 11 walls with street art stretching 10 miles along Dorset's coastline. Purbeck sculptor Jonathan Sells created the dual-statue outside the BIC which shows founder Lewis Tregonwell and today's Town Hall on one side, and Christopher Crabb Creeke (who rationalised the drainage) sat on a privy on the other. Fiona Kelly is a ceramics artist who has been making pots for over 40 years. Martyn Brewster is a leading abstract painter and printmaker whose work was the subject of a major travelling retrospective exhibition, launched at the Russell-Cotes in 1997. Bournemouth Arts Club has information about other local artists and their work.

Other street art you might see includes this in Exeter Crescent and the spectacular mural on the side of a building in Lansdowne Road (see Walk 2).

Maggy Howarth's pebble mosaic in The Square was inspired by the Bourne stream flowing beneath. The theme includes fish, mermaids and Neptune.

There is also a mural at Pokesdown train station.

During summer, look out for this Bournemouth Lion. Lions were installed in the town in 2011 before being auctioned for charity. This particular lion returned to its original site outside the Town Hall in June 2013.

Books and Authors

Particularly in the last century, Bournemouth became a favourite location for visiting artists and writers; presumably rarefied pine trees and sea views are inspirational. It thus has a rich literary past.

Mary Shelley (author of *Frankenstein*) is buried in St Peter's churchyard, in the family tomb, along with her parents, who were both writers, and reputedly the heart of her husband, the Romantic poet Percy Bysshe Shelley. Her father, William Godwin, was a political writer and novelist, a one-time Presbyterian priest who turned unbeliever, and was Percy's mentor. Mary's mother Mary Wollstonecraft was an Anglo-Irish feminist, famed for her *Vindication of the Rights of Woman* (1792). She married William in 1797 when already pregnant with Mary but died within 2 weeks of giving birth. Percy drowned off the coast of Italy in 1822 and many years later, Mary and Percy's son, Sir Percy

Florence Shelley, and his wife Jane, moved to Boscombe Manor, intending Mary to come and live with them. Alas, she died in 1851 before moving in.

Sir Henry Taylor, knighted for his work in the Colonial Office, came to Bournemouth in 1861, by which time he was famous as a dramatist. He welcomed many famous visitors to his home, The Roost, in today's Hinton Road, including Irish poet Aubrey de Vere and Alfred Lord Tennyson. A founder member and president of the Society for the Prevention of Cruelty to Animals, Sir Henry is also buried in St Peter's churchyard. His three daughters were all writers, with Una Taylor vividly describing life in Bournemouth in *Guests and Memories* (1925).

Charles Darwin rented Cliff Cottage, Exeter Road for a month in September 1862 to aid his son's convalescence after an attack of scarlet fever. The BIC occupies the site today.

Cliff Cottage in 1863. (Courtesy of Bournemouth Libraries.)

Lady Georgiana Fullerton lived at Ayrfield, St Peter's Road from 1877 to 1885 when she died. A well-known novelist and philanthropist, she founded St Joseph's Convalescent Home (now Meyrick Rise Care Home, 11–13 Branksome Wood Road) and St Walburga's School (on Mavis Road, still a Catholic primary school). There is a blue plaque on the Catholic Church on Richmond Hill commemorating her. Emma Marshall was a children's author of over 200 novels, including *Boscombe Chine: or, Fifty Years After. A Story* (1893), which pictures Bournemouth in 1838 and 1887, the years of Queen Victoria's Coronation and Jubilee.

The Earls of Malmesbury of Hurn Court published their memoirs. 2nd Earl, James Harris gave us *Half a Century of Sport in Hampshire* (published posthumously in 1905), while 3rd Earl, James Howard Harris, statesman and foreign secretary, published his *Memoirs of an Ex-Minister* in 1885.

Thomas Hardy used Bournemouth (under the name of 'Sandbourne') in both *Jude the Obscure* and *Tess of the D'Urbervilles*; Tess murders Alec in a Bournemouth boarding house (reputedly Brookside, now part of the Hermitage Hotel on Exeter Road). Sandbourne also appears in *The Hand of Ethelberta* and *A Tragedy of Two Ambitions*. It is portrayed as an exotic location, but also one of sin and shame. In July 1875, Hardy and first wife Emma spent 4 days in Bournemouth, during which time they took a boat from the pier to Swanage. He also attended the Winter Gardens in 1925 to see a musical setting to his play *The Famous Tragedy of the Queen of Cornwall*.

Paul Verlaine (1844–96) was a French poet, who, after release from Mons prison (charged with wounding and immorality), taught French and Latin at St Aloysius' College, 2 Westburn Terrace, Bournemouth, where he also completed one of his masterpieces (*Sagesse*), before returning to France. He worshipped at the Catholic Church of the Sacred Heart, Richmond Hill and wrote poems entitled *Bournemouth* and *La Mer de Bournemouth*. Nancy Meugens (1844–1933) was a prolific writer and translator, who was married to artist Arthur Bell and lived in Southbourne. Bournemouth-born composer Sir Hubert Parry is best known for his music, but he also wrote books, including *Evolution of the Art of Music* (1896).

Oscar Wilde arrived too late to give a scheduled recital at the Theatre Royal, Albert Road, in 1883, but dutifully returned the following week to make amends before a packed house. He stayed at the Royal Bath Hotel; Oscar's, the main restaurant there, contains mementoes. Wilde often visited Bournemouth.

Robert Louis Stevenson lived in Bournemouth between 1884 and 1887, moving to Skerryvore, Westbourne in April 1885, where he completed

Skerryvore House. (Courtesy of Bournemouth Libraries.)

A Child's Garden of Verses and wrote *The Strange Case of Dr Jekyll and Mr Hyde* and *Kidnapped*. A lifelong sufferer of TB, Stevenson was attracted by Bournemouth's healthy air. His collection of poems entitled *Underwoods* contains two poems about the house. Among the famous visitors to Skerryvore were authors Thomas Hardy and Henry James, for whom a special chair was kept. James is reputed to have said he found Bournemouth 'wholly uninteresting and almost

American in its newness and ugliness', but he kept coming back. Fellow TB sufferer William Ernest Henley was also a regular visitor, who collaborated on many plays with Stevenson. His poem *Invictus* (Unconquered) recurs in popular culture. William was one-legged and reputedly the inspiration for Stevenson's 'Long John Silver'.

Adeline Sergeant (1851–1904) was an English writer of over 90 novels, who died in Bournemouth, aged 53. She is buried in Wimborne Road Cemetery. Mary St Leger Kingsley (pseudonym Lucas Malet) was the daughter of Charles Kingsley and a novelist herself; her story *Adrian Savage* (1911) contains a full depiction of Bournemouth. Other early descriptions of the town include *Tracked Down* (Headon Hill, 1902), *The Lady of the Chine* (Margaret Scott Haycraft, c 1901), *Sinister Street, Volume 1* (Compton Mackenzie, 1914), *Jill-all-Alone* (Mrs Desmond Humphreys, 1914), *Allward* (Ethel Stefana Stevens, 1915) and *A Man and his Lesson* (William Babington Maxwell, 1919).

Beatrice Webb (1858–1943) was born into a wealthy Bournemouth family, but was always aware of the plight of the poor. She attended school on Bath Hill and Holy Trinity Church. She wrote the influential *The Co-operative Movement in Great Britain*, having researched the working class and trade unions. She was a prominent member of the Fabian Society and co-founder of *The New Statesman*. Beatrice returned to Bournemouth in the late 1880s, often staying at the Highcliff Hotel with husband Sydney Webb. She sometimes spoke in the town on poor law reform. Evelyn Sharp was an established author of children's fiction, a suffragist who became a militant suffragette, and editor of *Votes for Women* during WWI. In 1911 she addressed the Bournemouth branch of the Women's Social and Political Union. Two years later, militant suffragettes attacked Bournemouth pillar boxes.

D.H. Lawrence rewrote *The Trespasser* while boarding and recuperating from tubercular pneumonia at Compton House, St Peter's Road, early in 1912. Poet Rupert Brooke first came to Bournemouth aged nine and was a frequent visitor, as he had family living in town. He visited several times during WWI, attending Holy Trinity Church, Old Christchurch Road, for the last time in December 1914, before he died on the way to Gallipoli. Brooke joked he would 'expire vulgarly at Bournemouth and they will bury me on the shore by the bandstand'; instead his grave is on Skyros. The Rupert Brooke Memorial Garden in the Lower Gardens was established in 2014, marking the war's centenary.

Horace Annesley Vachell wrote several *Quinney* novels about an eponymous antiques dealer. Quinney's Hotel in Durley Road claims this was where the books were written. *Blinkers: A Romance of the Preconceived Idea* (1921) featured Bournemouth. Novelist and playwright John Galsworthy was a Bournemouth schoolboy, who went on to write *The Forsyte Saga* (1922). He attended Saugeen Primary School, Derby Road, as a 9-year-old, also singing in the choir at St Swithun's Church, Gervis Road. Flora Thompson, poet and author of *Lark Rise to Candleford*, lived in Winton, where two blue plaques commemorate her, at 4 Sedgley Road and 2 Edgehill Road.

Marguerite Radclyffe Hall (1880–1943), poet and author of the semi-autobiographical *The Well of Loneliness*, the first author to write a sympathetic study of lesbianism, was born in Durley Road at Sunny Lawn House, today's Durley Grange Hotel. *The Unlit Lamp* (1924) is a novel partly based in Bournemouth. Poet, playwright and acknowledged crime writer Dorothy L. Sayers gave birth to her son John Anthony Fleming in January 1924 at Tuckton Lodge, Iford Lane, Southbourne. Some of the most famous children's works of Enid Blyton were inspired by Dorset landscapes. She first visited Bournemouth during Easter 1931. Angela Brazil, one of the first British writers of 'modern schoolgirls' stories', based characters in *A Patriotic Schoolgirl* on family members who lived in St Catherine's Road, Southbourne.

Lawrence and Gerald Durrell have strong connections with Bournemouth. They first came to the area in 1931, when the family moved to Berridge House (Parkstone), before residing at 18 Wimborne Road (Dixie Lodge). Lawrence was a frequent visitor to Commin's bookshop, 100 Old Christchurch Road, run by Alan Gradon Thomas (president of the Antiquarian Booksellers' Association 1958/59). Lawrence married Nancy Myers in Bournemouth in 1935, and Gerald attended Wychwood School ('Witchwood' to Gerald) in Braidley Road, which he left after a beating from the headmaster. It was after this that the Durrells moved to Corfu (1935–39). Returning to England, mother Louisa bought a house at 52 St Albans Avenue, Charminster. The boys' sister Margaret Durrell (Margo), who later went on to write *Whatever Happened to Margo?* (1995), ran a boarding house across the road (No. 51). Gerald stayed at No. 51 and began writing *My Family and Other Animals* in the attic. His menagerie of 400 African and South American animals had a temporary home in Margo's garden and garage while he sought prospective sites for a zoo. They also had a spell in the basement of J.J. Allen (now House of Fraser), where one of the baboons escaped and wrecked a window display! During the war, Gerald worked on a farm in north Bournemouth (Longham). Lawrence meanwhile stayed at No. 52 with second wife Eve Cohen, 'en route' to Argentina for a new job.

Poet Cumberland Clark (the 'Bournemouth Bard') set up home in Bournemouth and wrote rhymes about the town, including *Bournemouth Song Book*. His life was ended when a German incendiary landed on his flat on 10 April 1941. Rev. J.D. Jones was minister at the Congregational Church, Richmond Hill from 1898 to 1937 and authored many devotional books and an autobiography, *Three Score Years and Ten* (1940). His volumes of sermons had large sales at home and abroad. There are many references to Bournemouth in the crime writing of Agatha Christie.

J.R.R. Tolkien regularly stayed at the Hotel Miramar from the 1950s to early 1970s, and retired here (he had a house called Woodridings on Lakeside Road in Poole, which has since been demolished) until his wife's death, when he returned to Oxford. Tolkien died on a visit to Bournemouth, but is buried in Oxford.

Tolkien always stayed in the same bedroom on the second floor, No. 37 then (today's No. 205) which has a splendid view over the bay.

Requiem for a Wren (1955) by Nevil Shute has much of the action set in and around the New Forest. When the Wren of the title meets her father in Bournemouth shortly before D-Day, it is at the Royal Bath Hotel, where he is receiving training as a member of the Royal Observer Corps.

Vera Chapman (1898–1996) was born in Bournemouth and wrote Arthurian novels. Gladys Mitchell (1901–83), writer of Mrs Bradley detective novels, retired to Dorset and Bournemouth featured in her books. Rupert Croft-Crooke was a prolific author of both fiction and non-fiction and resident of 4 Amira Court, Bourne Avenue. *The Green, Green Grass* was the last of his 24-volume autobiography, written in Bournemouth and published in 1977. Malcolm Muggeridge, journalist, author and satirist, wrote, in a class-conscious way, of Bournemouth in the 1930s, as a town without 'slums or proletariat'. John Creasey MBE (1908–73) was a crime and sci-fi writer, who wrote over 600 novels under 28 pseudonyms. He lived in Bournemouth for 20 years and tried, in vain, to become the town's Liberal MP. Dramatist Terence Rattigan (1911–77) set *Separate Tables*, televised plays by Noel Coward about life in a post-war guesthouse, in a Bournemouth hotel.

Mollie Moran lived in Bournemouth from the 1960s and published her memoir of working 'downstairs' (*Aprons and Silver Spoons*, 2013), shortly before she died. Anthony Burgess, author of *A Clockwork Orange*, married his first wife in Bournemouth in 1942. P.C. Wren, the author of *Beau Geste*, lived in the town. Frederick E. Smith is best known for his 1956 novel *633 Squadron*, which was made into a popular film. Smith lived for some 50 years in Southbourne, before dying in Bournemouth. Poet and author Rosemary Tonks moved to Bournemouth in 1979, staying here until she died.

Ian McQueen (1930–2011) was a local solicitor and author of *Bournemouth St Peter's* and *Sherlock Holmes Detected*. Ronald Hayman was born in Bournemouth and in *Secrets: Boyhood in a Jewish Hotel, 1932–1954* describes growing up in his gran's East Cliff Court Hotel. Bournemouth was once a favourite Jewish family holiday destination, with several kosher establishments in this area, perhaps because of the synagogue nearby on Old Christchurch Road (until *c.* 1962, the synagogue now being located at 53 Christchurch Road).

Dame Jane Goodall DBE, who also grew up in Bournemouth, is best known for her conservation work, especially with apes. She has also written over two-dozen books including children's books.

Alexis Lykiard's *Summer Ghosts* (1964) is partly based in Bournemouth. Gordon Williams is the Scottish author of *The Siege of Trencher's Farm*, which became the film *Straw Dogs*. Another of his novels was *The Upper Pleasure Garden* (1970), set in Bournemouth. Gordon Honeycombe (1936–2015), newscaster, author and playwright, lived in Crag Head flats, Manor Road, where he wrote his first books. Maggie Gee was born in Poole. Her *Light Years* (1985) is a novel partly set in Bournemouth. Douglas Adams set a scene from *The Hitch-Hiker's Guide to the Galaxy* on Bournemouth beach. Tricia Walker, author of *Benedict's Brother*, lives and works in Bournemouth. Louise Tondeur was born in Poole and grew up in Bournemouth. Her novel *The Water's Edge* is set in Bournemouth. Pauline Conolly's *The Water Doctor's Daughters*, the story of 19th-century homeopath and water-cure practitioner Dr James Marsden, has strong links to Bournemouth.

Other local authors include Stephen Clegg (*Maria's Papers*), Nick Churchill (*Yeah, Yeah, Yeah: the Beatles and Bournemouth*), Lucy Clarke (*Sea Sisters*), Elizabeth Darrell (*Max Rydal* crime series and historical fiction), Andrew Emery (*A History of Bournemouth Seafront*), Tobias Jones (*Blood on the Altar*, true crime), Jon Kremmer (*Bournemouth A Go! Go! A Sixties Memoir*), James Manlow (*Attraction*), Vincent May and Jan Marsh (*Bournemouth 1810–2010 from Smugglers to Surfers*), Imogen Parker (*The Time of our Lives*) and Martin Stratford (*Double Jeopardy*).

Travel Literature

Dr Augustus Granville wrote *The Spas of England* (1841), stating that 'Bourne' would become 'the very first watering place in England', having been delighted to find the waters 'quite free from any infiltration of dung'. *The Illustrated Historical and Picturesque Guide to Bournemouth* (1855) by Philip Brannon was the town's first substantial guidebook. One of his engravings was of the Rustic Bridge, erected in 1853; another was of the pier (still incomplete). An earlier guide (1842) by John Sydenham spoke of detached villas, ample gardens, shrubberies and walks, with a corroborative appendix supplied by Dr Thomas Aitken. Another man who helped put the town on the map was Dr Horace Dobell, extolling its virtues in *The Medical Aspects of Bournemouth and its Surroundings* (1885).

In Search of England (1927) by H.V. Morton has the author whimsical in the Lower Gardens when he witnesses a young lad sailing a boat in the Bourne stream. It appears to be Morton's own childhood being played back. Arthur Eperon's *Travellers' Britain* (1981) hits a nail squarely: 'Forget the bath chair image; the last one is in the museum.' Sometimes older books remind us of what is no more. Cliff Michelmore's *Holidays by Rail in Great Britain* (1986) lists a trio of lost museums: the Rothesay, Childhood and Big Four Railway. Bill Bryson was sub-editor at the *Echo* for 2 years in the 1970s. His *Notes from a Small Island* and *The Road to Little Dribbling* both mention the town. Sir Simon Jenkins' *England's Thousand Best Churches* (1999) includes a glowing tribute to St Peter's Church.

Keith Rawlings, former mayor of Bournemouth, wrote the book *Just Bournemouth* (2005) about the town and its inhabitants, while Rod Cooper (the mayor in 2013) extolls its virtues in *Discover Bournemouth*. In *Coast – Our Island Story* (2010), Nick Crane highlights Bournemouth as 'the most remarkable greenfield resort'. The Gardens are visited by Paul Gogarty in *The Coast Road* (2011), where he lauds Bournemouth as 'the quintessentially English smart resort'. He's also much enamoured of the Russell-Cotes. Matthew Engel (in *Engel's England*, 2014) observes quizzically that Bournemouth became more Hampshire than Dorset after the county boundary shifted. In *Channel Shore* (2015) Tom Fort reflects on Bournemouth's 'genteel charms' and some of its rich literary associations. *Pier Review* (2016) sees Jon Bounds and Danny Smith on a road trip to visit all English and Welsh piers. They particularly like Boscombe, 'one of the coolest in the country',

Music

Lt Dan Godfrey brought his Grenadier Band to Bournemouth in October 1893, and in 1896 the town became the first municipality in Britain to have a permanent orchestra, renamed as Bournemouth Symphony Orchestra (BSO). Lt Godfrey's son, Sir Dan Godfrey Jnr, was its first conductor and led the BSO for around 40 years.

Other conductors included Rudolf Schwarz, Constantin Silvestri and Sir Thomas Beecham. Sir Simon Rattle was assistant conductor in 1974. Even former PM Edward Heath had his moment at a fundraising concert in October 1975. The next longest-serving conductor after Sir Dan Godfrey Jnr is actually the present incumbent, Kirill Karabits, who has been principal conductor since 2009. Karabits was born in Kiev in 1976 and made his first appearance as conductor with the BSO in October 2006. The orchestra has appeared at the Promenade Concerts at the Royal Albert Hall and is now based in Poole.

The grave of Sir Dan Godfrey Jnr (1868– 1939) in St Peter's churchyard.

The BSO pictured in January 1912. (G.H. Stanford & Son photographer. Courtesy of Bournemouth Libraries.)

Sir Hubert Parry (1848–1918) was born at 2 Richmond Terrace, Richmond Hill, going on to compose the tune for *Jerusalem*. He became Head of the Royal College of Music and Professor of Music at Oxford.

The first Winter Gardens in Bournemouth was built as a glasshouse exhibition centre, resembling the Crystal Palace. It became a popular classical music venue with a capacity of 4000 from 1893. This coincided with the establishment of the Bournemouth Municipal Orchestra. The orchestra moved to the Pavilion in 1929 and the first Winter Gardens was demolished in 1935. The second Winter Gardens, a conventional brick building, was designed as a bowling alley. The building became a concert hall after WWII, known for its good acoustics. It was a popular pop/rock venue from the 1960s and the BSO was in residence until 1979, when it moved to the Lighthouse in Poole. By the 1990s the venue was in decline. It closed in 2002 and was demolished in 2006.

The first Winter Gardens (in existence 1875–1935). (J. Reade, Technical Photographer, Holdenhurst Road, Bournemouth. Courtesy of Bournemouth Libraries.)

Military bands still play at the bandstand in the Lower Gardens during the summer season. There is also a 1920s bandstand in Fisherman's Walk, which hosts various events throughout the year.

The Chines Hotel in Rosemount Road had its own basement jazz club, where both Oscar Peterson and John Dankworth are said to have performed. The Downstairs Club was launched in a basement too, at 9 Holdenhurst Road, in 1961 as another jazz club and became the town's first permanent rock venue (Le Disque a Go Go) in 1963. Well-known names performed here including instrumentalist Edward 'Tubby' Hayes and future superstars Manfred Mann, Eric Clapton, Georgie Fame, George Bruno 'Zoot' Money, Andy Summers and The Who. Another rock venue was the 'Ritz' (the 'Hive' from 1970, part of Starleys Hotel, one of the establishments that made way for the BIC), which began life as a 1950s ballroom before becoming a music venue in 1966. Acts included Jethro Tull, the Spencer Davis Group, Desmond Dekker, Fleetwood Mac, the Bee Gees, Thin Lizzy and Geno Washington.

The Beatles headlined a series of concerts at the Gaumont in August 1963, staying six nights at the Palace Court Hotel, during which they gave one of their first performances of *She Loves You*, just prior to its release. The photograph for the album cover 'With the Beatles' was taken in the Palace Court's dining room and George Harrison wrote his first Beatles' song *Don't Bother Me* there too. The Beatles also performed at the Winter Gardens in November 1963, highlights of which were transmitted coast-to-coast in the US the following week, and returned to the Gaumont in August (supported by The Kinks) and October 1964. The Beatles made a total of 16 appearances in Bournemouth and played more gigs at the Gaumont than any other concert venue in the UK, outside London.

The former Gaumont/Odeon in Westover Road.

Tony Blackburn (1943–) moved to Bournemouth aged three and would later take business studies at Bournemouth College. Before becoming a DJ he tried to pursue a singing career, his first performances being in Bournemouth (as vocalist with The Sabres). Peter Bellamy (1944–91), folk singer and interpreter of Rudyard Kipling's poems, was born in Bournemouth. Singer-songwriter Ralph McTell (1944–) lived in Southbourne in the early 1960s. Al Stewart (1945–), whose biggest hit was *Year of the Cat* (1976), worked in the linen department at Beales. One of his songs, *Foot of the Stage*, was inspired by the story of comedian Tony Hancock and inadvertently gave him the tune for *Year of the Cat*.

Ray Dorset (1946–), founder of Mungo Jerry, lives in the Westbourne area. Robert Fripp (1946–), King Crimson guitarist, attended Bournemouth College and performed at the Majestic Hotel. Musician-songwriter Gordon Haskell (1946–) was born in Bournemouth, as was Greg Lake (1947–2016). Steven Alexander 'Alex' James (1968–) was born in Boscombe and attended Bournemouth School for Boys. He is best known as the bassist of Blur. Choirmaster and broadcaster Gareth Malone (1975–) attended Bournemouth School for Boys and sang with the BSO's Symphony Chorus.

Other musicians with Bournemouth connections include Andy Summers (The Police guitarist), James McVey (The Vamps guitarist), Josh Devine (One Direction drummer), Amy Studt, Andrew Shatnyy, Denis Solomon, Jack Hawken, and Chris Moss Acid, and bands Electric Wizard, Air Traffic and Big Big Train.

Local radio station 2CR FM broadcast from studios in Southcote Road from 1980 until 2010, by which time it had become part of the Heart network. Former Radio 1 DJ Dave Lee Travis joined 2CR in 1993. Cliff Richard visited the studios in 1995, signing autographs outside.

Bournemouth has a great music scene today, with big acts appearing at the BIC, Bournemouth Pavilion and O2 Academy. Bournemouth Folk Club uses the Shelley Theatre as a venue. You can also enjoy local bands and DJs at numerous places including the Old Fire Station, with The Anvil rock bar opposite, O'Neill's, Smokin' Aces, Buffalo, Cameo, and Chaplin's and The Cellar Bar.

Award-winning Bournemouth Gilbert and Sullivan Productions (Bournemouth GaSP), formerly Bournemouth Gilbert and Sullivan Operatic Society, performs shows from Gilbert and Sullivan at major venues across Dorset and is expanding into grand opera and modern musicals. It is a charitable organisation which makes generous donations to local charities. Rehearsals are held at Iford United Reformed Church, Ropley Road.

Boscombe Light Opera Company was formed in 1954, and as today's Bournemouth and Boscombe Light Opera Company (BBLOC) is the town's biggest amateur musical theatre company. It currently stages a musical at the Pavilion Theatre and/or Christchurch's Regent Centre each year, as well as performing concerts in the area throughout the year, raising money for local good causes. BBLOC members have gone on to successful professional careers, most recently Jack Donnelly (who played the lead role of Jason in BBC's *Atlantis*) and Matt Jeans (who made his West End debut in the 2014 revival of *Miss Saigon*).

Dance and Drama

First, a little history. Stage actor-manager Sir Henry Irving (1838–1905) was a frequent visitor to Bournemouth, staying at the Royal Bath Hotel. There is an 'Irving Room' dedicated to him at the Russell-Cotes. Lillie Langtry (1853–1929), as well as being the paramour of Edward VII, was an actress and producer. In 1902 she received a royal command to perform in a play she co-wrote, *The Crossways*, before the King at Boscombe Theatre. Famous actress/theatre producer Olga Nethersole CBE (1867–1951) was born in London but lived in Bournemouth, where she died aged 83. Another actress, Dame Agnes 'Sybil' Thorndike (1882–1976), spent childhood holidays at Kinson

House, Horsham Avenue, accompanied by her younger brother, actor and writer Russell Thorndike, who wrote novels about a gentleman smuggler (*Dr Syn*).

Shelley Theatre has an interesting history. It was built in 1866 following an earlier timber theatre. The upper floor was added in 1870. Sir Percy Florence Shelley, only surviving son of Percy Bysshe Shelley and Mary Shelley, and his wife Jane had a passion for drama. They lived in Boscombe Manor (which dates to 1801), which became known as Shelley Manor, living there until 1899. Sadly, the manor was in a sorry state by 2005 but is now enjoying a new lease of life. Philip Proctor of Proctor Watts Cole Rutter (Chartered Architects) has overseen its restoration.

'Shelley Manor has been at the centre of Boscombe life from Sir Percy's days when he established it as a cultural hub. He loved the theatre and the one he established here has been described as "the most splendid private theatre in England". Percy enjoyed putting on topical, satirical plays, although his personal bent seemed to be more towards theatre mechanics and even painting the scenery! Lady Shelley didn't enjoy the best of health and she liked to watch the productions from her bedroom, where she had a hatch, looking out at the stage, which still exists. The Shelleys' philanthropy manifested itself in the Boscombe Carnivals, held in the grounds of the manor, and the theatricals, which not only entertained, but raised funds for medical services in Boscombe.

In 1911 the house became a girl's school, Grovely Manor. It also served time as a Home Guard centre and, post-war, the further education college. An integral part of the site's regeneration was the opening of the Shelley Manor Medical Centre here in 2009 (the Inner Sanctum where Percy Bysshe Shelley's heart once resided for 50 years is now Consulting Room 2!). Given the Shelleys' notable health projects, it feels like affairs have now gone full circle. Then, the re-opening

of the 160-seat theatre was achieved in October 2010 with a candlelit production of Frankenstein – the Year without a Summer, *an apt opening night if ever there was one! The Shelley Theatre Trust launched its first programme in 2014 and we are proud of what has been achieved in restoring it to its former glory, and it is fantastic that the theatre, so loved by Sir Percy and Lady Shelley, is once again entertaining Bournemouth audiences.'*

Bournemouth Amateur Dramatic Society (BADS) was formed in 1876 and at one time had Sir Percy Shelley as President. The oldest amateur drama club in the town today is Bournemouth Little Theatre Club (BLTC), founded in 1919, which still performs at Jameson Road, Winton. The BLTC created the Palace Court Theatre in Hinton Road in 1931 and it became a focal point for local drama. However, there was increasing competition and by the 1960s it became too expensive to run. It was sold to LM Theatres in 1970 and the lower ground floor was converted into the Galaxy Cinema, and the main 595-seat theatre upstairs was renamed the Playhouse. Eventually both sections were run as cinemas. There was a brief reprieve in 1983 when it staged Joseph, but productions eventually ceased in 1987. After much planning debate about its future use, in 1990 it was sold and became a church – the Wessex Christian Centre. In sympathy they retained many of the theatrical features. The 900-seat Pier Theatre opened its doors in 1960, once the pier head had been reinforced with a new concrete base to take the weight. It closed in 2012.

Bournemouth Pavilion's Theatre and Ballroom is a traditional venue for year-round entertainment. Built in the 1920s, it was refurbished in 2007 and holds an audience of 1012 in fixed seats on a raked floor with a further 446 in the circle. It retains its splendour and elegant styling and is Bournemouth's regular home for West End stage shows, opera, ballet, pantomime and comedy, as well as for corporate presentations and dinner dances, product launches, fashion shows and small conferences, complementing what goes on at the BIC. Pavilion Dance South West at the back of the Pavilion offers live performances, screenings, exhibitions and more than 40 dance classes a week.

Film and TV

East Cliff Cottage, built in 1895, is now a hotel.

James Stewart, or 'Stewart Granger' (1913–93) was an English film star, whose childhood home was East Cliff Cottage on Grove Road, which was owned by his mother until 1979. Sir Alec Guinness (1914–2000) went to school in Southbourne, where the headmaster apparently said he'd never make an actor! Later he stayed regularly with his aunt and uncle in Westbourne, where his grandfather had been the arcade caretaker.

Actor and comedian Tony Hancock (1924–68) was brought up in Bournemouth from the age of three. His father (also a comedian and entertainer) ran the Railway Hotel, Holdenhurst Road. After his father died, Hancock lived with the rest of the family at the Durlston Court Hotel, Gervis Road, and later attended Bournemouth College. His first engagement was entertaining troops at the Church of the Sacred Heart, Richmond Hill, in 1940. Hancock's first paid gig was at the Avon Social Club, 51 Avon Road, Springbourne. Fellow comedian and actor Benny Hill attended Bournemouth School for Boys when his school evacuated there during WWII. Other former pupils include actor Charles Gray, who played arch-villain Blofeld in *Diamonds Are Forever* and made his stage debut in Westover Road; journalist and TV presenter Mark Austin, who began his media career as a general reporter on the *Echo* (1976–80); and actor Christian Bale (*Batman*).

Dame Jane Goodall (animal conservationist considered the world's foremost expert on chimpanzees) moved to Bournemouth aged 12, and still has a home, The Birches, in the town. She has made many films over a 50-year period.

The 1963 film of Edgar Wallace's novel *To Have and to Hold* was filmed in Bournemouth, after producer Jack Greenwood honeymooned in the town and liked it! In the 1967 film *Valentino*, the Russell-Cotes doubled as Valentino's Hollywood home. *Cause Célèbre* (1989) told the story of the Rattenbury murder that occurred in Manor Road, with Helen Mirren starring as Alma Rattenbury and Harry Andrews playing the role of her doomed husband. Popular BBC TV series *One Foot in the Grave* had some scenes filmed in Bournemouth. Channel 4's *Demolition* (2005) featured the Waterfront complex with its IMAX cinema as one of its dozen architectural eyesores; in fact, a poll conducted by the programme revealed it was the most hated building in England!

In 2006 the former Tollard Royal Hotel (today's Tollard Court apartments) was featured on *Grand Designs* when the roof flat/penthouse was converted. The nightclub scene in Guy Ritchie's *RocknRolla* (2008) was filmed at The Old Fire Station.

In Series 3 of *Great British Railway Journeys* (2012) Michael Portillo spoke to local historian Andrew Emery in the Pleasure Gardens and took a ride on a 1908 cliff lift. Portillo returned in Series 9 (2018) when he was on the trail of Edward VII and discovered Bournemouth's beach hut history. *K-Shop* (2016, a modern take on *Sweeney Todd*) was filmed in and around Bournemouth. TV-host Stephen Mulhern filmed game show *In for a Penny* in Bournemouth in August 2018.

Besides the large Odeon cinema near The Square and the Shelley Theatre, where else can you catch a film? Westbourne Arcade contains many hidden treasures, one of which is The Vintage Lounge, a welcoming café run by Annalise Hill. Downstairs you'll find a little bit of cinematographic history, for here is the 'Colosseum', the UK's smallest permanent cinema. Paul Whitehouse has been the owner since 2013.

'When I bought the business, we had a ground floor café and homeware shop. The idea of the cinema came to me when I was watching a TV programme about Wales, featuring a railway carriage that had been converted to a cinema. The "Colosseum" opened in 2014 as a local suburbia cinema. We've certainly attracted some publicity, for example, we had a coach party from Manchester visit us, which meant having to do two screenings! We operate in a niche market, showing foreign films, films our customers bring in, or ones we're able to hire for

The main auditorium in the Colosseum has just 19 seats, including a two-seater 'royal box'.

them. We've also put on digital theatre (live theatre showings). On one occasion we had a breakfast screening of the Australian Open tennis final. We're open five days a week, plus we do private hire, for example, children's parties, birthday gatherings and company training days. Every day is different and one of the perks is the number of interesting people we have come in. We're trying to enhance the authentic feel of the place with, for example, the "Picturegoer" posters, and the bar area is being redecorated with a more Victorian-nostalgic décor. It is a very intimate experience, but very much a one-man-show, so whoever is on duty is projectionist, bar-steward, usherette and so forth! The evolution of the cinema has been fascinating, with a further step achieved in 2017 when we opened a new 8-seat cinema in the old store room, complete with reclining leather seats. I guess that makes us the smallest and the second-smallest!'

Folklore and Characters

Things that Go 'Bump'

There are far fewer ghost stories in Bournemouth than neighbouring Christchurch, perhaps due to the former's relative immaturity. Perhaps the most famous is the poltergeist of Abbott Road, Winton, which went on a wrecking-spree at No. 37 in 1981. The drama began on Friday 14 August, at around 9 am, when furniture was overturned and other items such as vases and crockery went flying in the Burden family home. Police were called and witnessed further destruction as the kitchen cabinet went over, spilling its contents on the floor. A service of exorcism was conducted the same day, followed by a séance, but the activity began again at around the same time the following morning. Interestingly, when the Burdens' 8-year-old son Bradley went across the road to a neighbour's, the disturbances ceased. There was a further bout later that morning, this time witnessed by a social worker. Another séance was held, and the family was advised to vacate the house for 4 days, by which time the story had become headline news. Whether the second séance was the catalyst we'll never know, but there was no further reported activity.

Bournemouth's Town Hall was formerly a military hospital and is reputedly haunted by a WWI soldier, who appears each October 31st. There is also said to be a ghostly moggy, plus spectral horses and carriages have been seen outside, presumably still bringing those hotel guests from its Mont Dore days. Talbot Woods is said to be haunted by a large hound, while the area around Millhams Road, between Kinson and Longham, is said to be the patch of a 'white lady', allegedly killed by a horse and trap while walking this road.

Gullivers Tavern in Kinson (now the Acorn Pub) was the scene of a reported haunting in the 1980s (a man, presumably a smuggler, sat on a chest, counting his ill-gotten gains). The area around St Andrew's Church on Millhams Road is also said to be haunted by smugglers. There is a story about a ghostly rider on Hengistbury Head, allegedly sighted in 1982, with 17th-century-style jacket and collar-length hair; perhaps a little early to be a smuggler.

Ghosts have been sighted by nurses in the Shelley Medical Centre, and a lady in black was seen to defend the staircase on the stage during a performance at the Shelley Theatre. Boscombe's Grand Theatre (today's O2 Academy) has reported ghostly sightings (a clown, mysterious applause when the building was empty, a girl running, small stones being thrown, and an odd blurred red light). Langtry Manor is said to be haunted by Lillie Langtry, particularly when it's time for high tea, and a carriage containing the Prince of Wales and Lillie is sometimes said to draw up outside.

Lillie's house is now the Langtry Manor Hotel, and Langtry House next door, built by Lillie for her mother, is now apartments.

Villa Madeira in Manor Road, scene of the Rattenbury murder, is allegedly haunted by both a slim figure in the garden (Alma?) and an elderly man walking past the house, which it has been suggested could be George Stoner returning to the scene of his crime. The ghost of lawyer Edmund Bott, a former inhabitant of Stourfield House, was allegedly seen driving a coach and four after his death in 1788. There have been ghostly sightings at Throop Mill, including black-coated figures (possibly monks) and laughter and song from long-dead children (said to have been lost in an accident in the 1800s). An eyewitness claimed to have seen a little girl in Victorian dress in both 2004 and 2012, with the attendant sound of crying.

Creatures

In 1851 a sturgeon was caught in the River Stour at Iford, measuring over 7 ft long and weighing a colossal 109 lb. At the turn of the 20th century, the skeleton of the 'Boscombe Whale' (a 65- to 70-ft long, 40-ton North Atlantic whale), which was stranded on the beach in January 1897, was exhibited on Boscombe Pier. It required a specially built metal framework to hold it together and exhibit it safely and was a big draw for several years (until 1904). In 1915, another marine creature to cause a stir was a 4½-ft-long porpoise, which was washed up on East Cliff beach; it had been killed by a boat propeller. In 1970, dolphins began a 3-month staycation as a tourist attraction on the seafront at Durley Chine (in a 10-ft-deep tank). 'Sammy the Seal' was here in 1971, napping on the beach at Alum Chine and then spotted at Durley Chine. In 1979, sea lions from the Pier's Aqua Show were billeted at Stokewood Road baths, where they kept residents awake.

River Stour at Iford

After WW I there was clearly a rat problem, as the council launched its 'Swat the Rat' campaign in 1919. That's probably not the case now as it was revealed in February 2018 that Bournemouth has the highest concentration of urban foxes in the UK, with 23 per km^2 (in London, the figure is 18).

Murders and Deaths

A path leading down to the sea from Clifton Road, Southbourne is known locally as Mount Misery. The name may derive from the difficulty here of clambering down the rocky cliffs, but another explanation is that of a young

Grave of Frederick Abberline, Chief Inspector CID Scotland Yard (1843–1929).

girl who committed suicide by leaping from the cliff after witnessing the death of her smuggler lover when his boat was wrecked. The sister of John Wilkes Booth, who assassinated President Lincoln, Asia Booth Clarke (1835–88), lived in Bournemouth and wrote *John Wilkes Booth: A Sister's Memoir*. Montague Druitt was one of the prime suspects in the Jack the Ripper murders, his death from drowning in the Thames (December 1888) coinciding with the end of the serial killings. He was the younger brother of William H. Druitt, a solicitor living in Bournemouth. Montague stayed with his brother for a night towards the end of October 1888. Frederick Abberline, one of the investigating officers, was born in Blandford, retired to 195 Holdenhurst Road, Bournemouth, and is buried in Wimborne Road Cemetery.

Emma Sherriff, a 36-year-old dressmaker, who lived in Palmerston Road, Boscombe, was found murdered on the cliffs at Southbourne in February 1908. Male acquaintance John Francis McGuire (21), who had deserted the Army in 1906, was in financial difficulty, and a beneficiary of the victim's will. He was accused of the murder, but, with a key-witness continually changing her evidence, charges were dropped.

In December 1921, Irene Wilkins, aged 31, arrived at Bournemouth station from Waterloo for a bogus job interview. Her body was found in Tuckton the following day and chauffeur Thomas Allaway was hanged for her murder. One of Bournemouth's more famous murders was that of 67-year-old architect Francis Rattenbury in 1935, which occurred at 5 Manor Road. His wife Alma (31) was found not guilty of murder, but her lover George Stoner (19) was. Consumed with grief, Alma took her own life at the Three Arches bridge beside the River Avon in Christchurch, while Stoner's death sentence was commuted to 'life', of which he served only 7 years.

Perhaps the most notorious murderer associated with Bournemouth was Neville Heath, who killed two women: one in London and the second in Bournemouth. Heath met holidaymaker Doreen Marshall in the town in July 1946. Heath was staying at the Tollard Royal Hotel, while Marshall was at the Norfolk on Richmond Hill. Her body was found in Branksome Dene Chine. Heath was executed in October 1946.

In May 1954, 74-year-old Amy Lloyd was found murdered at her home in Richmond Park Avenue. The culprit was a 16-year-old juvenile Air Scout who served 'some years' before release. A more recent unsolved murder, in May 1986, was that of Sandra Court, who had been celebrating her last day of employment in Holdenhurst Road before taking a new job in Majorca. Her body was found north of the town, on the Avon Causeway.

The IRA planted eight bombs around Bournemouth in August 1993, of which five detonated. The attack destroyed one shop and caused other structural damage, including to Bournemouth Pier, plus some minor injuries.

Characters

The Countess of Strathmore and Kinghorne, Mary Bowes (1749–1800), a tenant at Stourfield House, liked to set places for her pet dogs at the dinner table apparently. 'The Chinese Giant' Zhan Shichai (c 1841–93) made a living as a 'curiosity' under various stage names, including Chang Woo Gow. He toured many countries, including America with the famous Barnum's Greatest Show on Earth, with whom he earned up to $500 per month. Much later, in 1890, he came to Bournemouth for his health, suffering from TB, living first in Derby Road, then moving to 'Moyuen', 6 Southcote Road, Boscombe, a new Victorian villa near the station (now the Ashleigh Hotel). He opened

Zhan (c 1870) was approximately 8 ft tall and weighed 26 stone. (Copyright Ralph Repo, Wikimedia Commons.)

a Chinese teahouse and a store selling Chinese imports. He was a gentle giant and, unable to avoid onlookers, would kindly indulge them by lighting a cigar from one of the gas lamps, while strolling through the town. He is buried in Wimborne Road Cemetery in an unmarked grave (possibly at his request to end a lifetime of gawping); his coffin was 8 ft 6 inches long. His friendly spirit is said to haunt the Ashleigh.

Dr Cornelius Herz was implicated in the Panama scandals, a corruption linked to the building of the Panama Canal which erupted in France in 1892. Herz was living in a house belonging to Sir Henry Drummond Wolff ('Tankerville' on Owls Road) in Boscombe at the time, which unwittingly became the scene of extradition proceedings. Barbara Joyce Dainton, née West was born in Bournemouth and found unwanted fame as the penultimate remaining survivor of the sinking of *RMS Titanic* in April 1912. She was 10 months old and was rescued along with her mother and sister. Her father died in the tragedy. All her life Barbara refused to have anything to do with 'the Titanic people'. Horatio Bottomley, editor of *John Bull*, was an MP either side of WWI, who engaged in patriotic oratory during the war. He spoke at the Winter Gardens in September 1915, one of his 'music hall engagements disguised as recruiting meetings'. He presided over a mock trial of the Kaiser. Bottomley was convicted of fraud in 1922, serving 5 years of a 7-year sentence.

Doreen Valiente (1922–99) was an English Wiccan (pagan witch) and writer, who composed much of the early *Gardnerian* (after Gerald Gardner) religious liturgy. She developed her interest in the occult after WWII and began practicing ceremonial magic while living in Bournemouth. Leading British art historian and Surveyor of the Queen's Pictures Anthony Blunt (1907–83) was also a spy working for the Soviet Union during the Cold War. He was brought up in Bournemouth, where his father was vicar of Holy Trinity Church. In the wake of the Profumo affair, a British political scandal of the early 1960s, showgirl models Christine Keeler and Mandy Rice-Davies fled to Bournemouth to escape press attention. They hid out in a rented flat in Talbot Woods. A tip-off led to the arrest of two of the Great Train Robbers, Roger Cordrey and William Boal, in Tweedale Road, a quiet cul-de-sac off Broadway Lane on the north side of Castle Lane, in 1963. Police found vehicles containing around £100,000 and confirmed the two men had been staying in a flat above a florist in Wimborne Road, Moordown. It was the first substantial sum to be recovered.

Other Oddities

A popular song sung by local children in the late 18th century is of 'a battle' that was 'fought at Tuckton Cross, where Wick won and Tuckton lost'. The scrap was between two youths, both of whom fancied a local girl – the maid of Mrs Edmund Bott from Stourfield House. The winner lived in Wick. In 1871 the remnants of over 30 trees were found in the shallows west of Bournemouth Pier, the fossilised remains of a once-mighty forest which might have extended far out into the bay. The trees were identified as ancient specimens of common fir (*Pinus sylvestris*). One evening in the late 1800s when *The Wreck Ashore* (a drama in two acts by John Baldwin Buckstone) was being performed at Shelley Theatre, fact and fiction coalesced when a shipwrecked Norwegian sailor was carried into the house after his vessel had been driven onto the beach. As a humorous aside, the author and his wife were married in the Registry Office, Old Christchurch Road, in 1984. The building (Cren Dahr, No. 159) found an interesting afterlife as a gentlemen's club 'Wiggle'!

Family Fun and Other Activities

Boating and Ferries

In the past, Bournemouth Pier has been a departure point for a mixture of pleasure boat rides, as well as a 'white-knuckle' powerboat experience. However, there hasn't been a regular operator at the pier since 2013. There are boats for hire at Tuckton Tea Gardens. Wick Ferry at the eastern end of the Gardens takes passengers the short distance across the river to the Captain's Club Hotel (Christchurch). Larger ferries ply the River Stour to Christchurch's Town Quay and the sand spit at Hengistbury Head, and Mudeford Ferry also connects Mudeford Quay with the spit.

Bournemouth Aviary

The first aviary was built in Pine Walk in the Lower Gardens in the 1930s, while the current design dates back before 1950. It can be visited at any time, free of charge. Originally maintained by the council, it is now run entirely by volunteers. Most of the birds are rescued, with a few born in the aviary. A new design for the aviary has been proposed that will incorporate more flight space and 360-degree viewing.

Pier Approach – Big Wheel and Aquarium

The Big Wheel at the Pier Approach takes customers up to 100 ft into the air. The Oceanarium (Bournemouth Aquarium) offers visitors a journey around the waters of the world, where you can see sharks, sea turtles, stingrays, dwarf crocodiles, jellyfish, clownfish, Inca terns, penguins and otters. There are up to nine feeding presentations a day. The Oceanarium is open every day except Christmas Day and has a café and shop.

City Sightseeing Bournemouth

A discounted bus and boat combo ticket includes an open-top bus tour between Bournemouth Pier and Poole Quay and back, plus the opportunity to hop on and off a number of boat services within 24 hours. See www.citysightseeing-bournemouth.co.uk for details.

Land Trains

Land trains operate along the seafront, one from Bournemouth Pier to Branksome Chine, the other from Bournemouth Pier to Boscombe's Manor Steps and Beach pods, returning via Boscombe Precinct and Gardens over the East Overcliff. Trains run daily between April and October, during school holidays and at winter weekends. There is a lengthy, purpose-built train garage/shed just west of Boscombe pier, disguised (painted) with a beach hut design. The much-admired land ('Noddy') train at Hengistbury Head was started by the Faris family in 1969 and operated by them for 45 years. The council's decision not to renew their licence and operate the train themselves was greeted with considerable angst. An unfortunate incident involving a cyclist in late 2018 and the subsequent HSE enquiry caused a lengthy closure,

but the train generally operates between the Hiker Café and Mudeford Spit every day except Christmas Day.

Miniature Railway

The Bournemouth & District Society of Model Engineers (B&DSME) was formed in 1924, and from 1966 operated a miniature railway at Kings Park for 35 years. Expansion of the AFC Bournemouth football stadium forced a move to the current Littledown Park location in 2004. The new dog-bone-shaped track is generally open to the public on Sunday and Wednesday, weather dependent. It can run 7.25, 5 and 3.5 inch gauge locomotives and is suitable for passenger hauling, so family rides are available.

George Wheatley was a long-standing member of the B&DSME, seen here driving his Sweet Pea 5-inch gauge locomotive named Sarie Marais. (Courtesy of Littledown Railway, operated by B&DSME.)

Play Areas

Outdoor play areas in Bournemouth include ones at Alum Chine, Boscombe Chine Gardens, Central Gardens (adjacent to the tennis centre), Churchill Gardens (once the playing fields of Gorse Cliff School, Boscombe), Fisherman's Walk (Southbourne), Iford Playing Fields, Kings Park Playground, Kinson Common, Littledown Park, Moordown

Recreation Ground, Moore Avenue Park (West Howe), Muscliff Park, Noyce Gardens (Townsend), Pelhams Park, Poole Lane (West Howe), Queens Park, Redhill Park, Seafield Gardens (Southbourne), Setley Gardens (near Castlepoint, Castle Lane West), Slades Farm (Ensbury Park), Springbourne Library Gardens (Holdenhurst Road), The Rookery (off Cranleigh Road, Southbourne), Tuckton Gardens (Wick Lane) and Winton Recreation Ground.

Mr Mulligans restaurant and bars in the BH2 (Odeon) Leisure Complex has adventure golf featuring three courses with exciting on-course immersive technology, suitable for all ages. 'Mighty Claws Adventure Golf' is located with Playgolf on Riverside Avenue; here you come face to face with moving dinosaurs and can enjoy a bite to eat yourself at the Kitchen Club. There is also dinosaur-themed crazy golf. Smugglers' Cove Adventure Golf at Pier Approach transports you back to the 1700s, and there is more crazy golf in the Lower Gardens and Tuckton Tea Gardens, where there is also putting.

Bournemouth Lower Gardens Classic Mini Golf.

Oasis Fun on Glen Fern Road is open 7 days a week and includes a six-lane bowling alley, soft play centre, large adventure golf course, arcades and pool tables. Refreshments are available at an American diner and bar. Extending more than 1 km either side of Boscombe Pier, Coastal Activity Park has over 30 different activities, including everything from sports courts to water sports. Have a try at 'slacklining' on the full-time facility. Littledown Centre is a large leisure centre which has the Altitude High Ropes Adventure leisure attraction and acres of parkland to explore, including a lake, miniature steam railway and ride-on trains.

High ropes course and zip-line over the lake at Littledown Centre.

Kings Park Skate Park is next to the athletics stadium, accessible from either Ashley Road or Gloucester Road. Slades Farm at Ensbury Park is a popular play area, with a play trail, zip-line and treehouse.

Slades Farm skate park is also suitable for roller blading and BMX.

Youth Centres and Groups

The YMCA was formed in 1844, but Bournemouth's first centre didn't arrive until 1879, when it was established in rented rooms above JE Beale's shop in Old Christchurch Road; it then moved to rented accommodation in St Peter's Road in the early 1880s, before settling in the purpose-built Cairns Memorial Hall in 1886. A hostel and one of the country's first gymnasiums were added in the early 1900s. The move to its current site between Westover Road and Hinton Road came in 1930. Improvements and expansion continue, and there are local partnerships in Pokesdown, Winton, Broadstone and Townsend, plus an Activity Centre in Studland on the Isle of Purbeck.

Some boys from Bournemouth Boys' Brigade took part in the very first Scout camp on Brownsea Island, Poole Harbour, in July/August 1907. The experimental camp involved 20 boys from widely different backgrounds (Eton, Harrow, London's East End and the Bournemouth area). Much of the preparation fell to Captain Henry Robson of Bournemouth Boys' Brigade, who owned a grocery business in The Triangle. Bournemouth Scouts has some 1,600 members today.

Pokesdown Youth Centre continues to operate in Stourvale Road, Southbourne and is one of the oldest in the country, having been in existence for over 100 years. Fusion Youth Club is in the town centre, tucked away in Old Christchurch Lane. Townsend Youth Centre is located in Townsend Housing Community on the town's northern outskirts. Embassy Youth Centre is in Brassey Road (Winton/Moordown). The '507' at 507 Christchurch Road, Boscombe provides help and support to 13- to 19-year-olds. 'Sussed' is based in Wimborne Road, Kinson and acts as an information, advice and guidance hub supporting young people aged 13–19. It provides a safe, friendly, non-judgemental environment to gain support for any issues affecting them. Youth workers, advisors and sexual health nurses are available to give information, advice and guidance on benefits, discrimination, health and care, housing, relationships, training and back to work.

Bournemouth Pier

The current pier has undergone many changes over the years. The challenge today is to preserve an iconic structure while also providing activities that people expect this century. Rory Holburn is director of 'Openwide', a family-oriented entertainments producer that won the tender in 2006 to run the pier's visitor attractions. At the time, this comprised a theatre, Key West café, ground-floor trading units and children's fun-fare.

'When we took over, the Pier Theatre and Key West were both rundown. We wanted to bring the theatre space back to life and tried to make the theatre work for several years. We then put "RockReef" in there in May 2013, which has a selection of clip 'n climb climbing walls, HighLine, vertical slides, "leap of faith" and caving – an indoor, all-year, all-weather facility. RockReef has done remarkably well. We also cater for parties (minimum ten people) and there's a café in there too.

Then in September 2013 we added the outside Zip Line, the world's first and only pier to shore zip-wire. You don't need to be an extreme sports enthusiast to try the zip-wire. We've had people in their 90s trying it. There are no age limits as such; just height and weight restrictions. This is all part of our rigorous attention to health and safety. Newly married couples have celebrated their marriage by taking on the zip-wire and we've had our share of famous customers too, everyone from the "Cherries" players and the British Army's Red Devils Parachute Regiment Display Team to "X Factor" contestant Max Stone and actress and all-round entertainer Debra Stephenson. After completing the zip-wire, people (famous or not) might want to relax with some refreshments in "Key West", enjoying the amazing panorama.

We aim to promote the pier as a single visitor attraction and will forever be looking to refresh what it offers, whilst respecting the unique heritage that we have here. It's very important that we keep the community onside with our use of what is an iconic structure; however, I firmly believe that we've been able to give it a new lease of life.'

Sport and Leisure

Note: Many sports have relocated to Bournemouth Sports Club at Chapel Gate, East Parley; this is near the airport and actually in Christchurch borough, but they are still classed as 'Bournemouth' sports for the purposes of this book.

Water Sports

As long ago as 1849, a Bournemouth and Poole Regatta was held, with yacht races taking place for the Canford Cup, engraved '*Poole Regatta*'. The coastline remains a magnet for sailors, but Bournemouth obviously has no harbour, and emphasis is now more on Poole for racing.

Bournemouth Rowing Club (formerly Westover and Bournemouth) was established in 1865 and is one of the oldest coastal rowing clubs in the south and the oldest sporting club in Dorset. The Westover club (1871) and Bournemouth club appear to have been bitter rivals until they amalgamated. A coastal rowing regatta (established in 1869) is generally held each summer, on a 1,000-m course between the end of the Pier and level with Durley Chine. The seafront clubhouse was demolished in 2012 to make way for the Oceanarium expansion. A rowing club also emerged in Boscombe in 1912, and a Surf Boat Club started in 2012, operating from Bournemouth Sea Cadet Compound on Iford Lane.

Bournemouth Rowing Club on the River Stour at Tuckton.

Boscombe Surf Reef, the first artificial surfing reef constructed in the northern hemisphere, was installed in 2009 near Boscombe Pier to enhance surfing conditions. After many technical and contractual difficulties, the reef was rebranded as a 'coastal activity park' (2014), concentrating on snorkelling, diving, wind and kite surfing, as well as onshore sports.

Powerboat P1 'Superstock' Championships take place, close to shore, on a two nautical mile course, with races lasting 20–30 minutes. Aqua X Jet Ski Championships run alongside the Superstock series.

John MacGregor (1825–92), nicknamed Rob Roy, is generally credited with development of the first sailing canoes and with popularising canoeing as a sport in Europe and the US. He founded, and was first Captain of, the British Royal Canoe Club, and was the author of *A Thousand Miles in the Rob Roy Canoe*. He died in Boscombe, aged 67, and is buried in Wimborne Road Cemetery.

Hengistbury Head Outdoor Education Centre (OEC) overlooking Stanpit Marsh is ideally situated for learning to sail in Christchurch Harbour's shallow, safe waters. It has a variety of boats to suit all ages and levels of sailing experience and offers courses leading to RYA qualifications. Other activities include windsurfing, paddlesports, powerboating, rowing and multi-activity days.

The OEC tucked away in Wick Fields on the edge of Christchurch Harbour.

Fishing

Fishing is popular at Hengistbury Head (sea fishing), off both piers, at Iford Meadows, Stour Valley Nature Reserve and Millhams Mead (Longham). Fish caught from the sea include bass, plaice, grey mullet, mackerel, tope, skate and sea bream. A guide of 1874 mentions fishermen catching 'enormous shoals' of mackerel and herring, while children fished off the pier for smelts and whiting (1899). Southbourne Pier was another good spot for catching plaice, turbot and bass in the 1890s, while Middle and Durley Chine beaches were good for whiting. A spot near the Whiting Rocks (opposite Durley Chine) is often mentioned as the best place to fish. There used to be a Bournemouth Annual Fishing Festival in the autumn (the Open Boat Fishing Festival). When Boscombe and Southbourne Sea Fishing Club was founded in 1918, its first president was Harry Selfridge (founder of the department store), who was at the time a tenant at Highcliffe Castle in Christchurch.

Football

AFC Bournemouth ('the Cherries') dates from 1899, formed from leftovers of the disbanded Boscombe St John's Lads Institute FC. Its original name was Boscombe FC and it moved to Kings Park in 1910, attaining Football League status in 1923. The 'Cherries' nickname came from either cherry orchards on the Cooper-Dean estate (the club's Dean Court ground was adjacent) or the cherry-red striped shirts worn by the early sides. The club once had the longest name in the League (Bournemouth and Boscombe Athletic Football Club).

For most of its existence the club operated in the League's lower divisions, except for 1987–90 when it spent three seasons in Division 2 under Harry Redknapp. This achievement was surpassed more recently by attaining the Premiership in 2015 under Eddie Howe, a turn of events unforeseen in 1910, when it was stated that 'Geographically situated as we are, it is very doubtful if a professional team of any consequence will ever be established here' (*Bournemouth: The Biography*). The club has also enjoyed some success in cup competitions, including reaching the FA Cup quarter-final in 1956–57,

AFC Bournemouth's 11,450-capacity Vitality stadium in Kings Park. It was completely rebuilt in 2001 – the pitch was rotated 90 degrees and moved away from adjacent housing, but it's the smallest in the Premier League. Ongoing success in the Premier League makes a new stadium almost inevitable.

losing to Manchester United before a record 28,799 crowd at the former Dean Court ground. The club also reached the Auto-Windscreen Shield final at Wembley in 1997–98. George Best played five games for the team in 1983. In 1996, when AFC Bournemouth came within a quarter-of-an-hour of being wound up, it was saved by a supporters' trust fund, which injected vital cash into the club when it was most desperately needed, and led to the creation of one of the first (if not the first) of Europe's community clubs (where the club is owned, or majority-owned, by its supporters).

Many are unaware there is another, older Bournemouth football club, Bournemouth FC ('the Poppies'). It was a merger with another club, Bournemouth Wanderers, which prompted a change of colours from green and white hoops to today's all red (hence 'the Poppies'). Past presidents have included William Pickford, who was also President of the Football Association, and Derek Nippard, who refereed the 1978 FA Cup Final. Current chairman Bob Corbin has been associated with the club since 1986.

'It's a difficult job being chairman of a small club such as the Poppies. I've put a few bob in over the years and I don't expect to see a return on my investment! There are seven or eight of us who effectively keep the club going, with others pitching in from time to time. Our attendances average around 45, which illustrates what we're up against. We've had some great times here though. I remember the friendly games against the Cherries particularly. On one occasion we actually beat them 2–1, but the result was misreported in the local press. I guess no-one could actually credit that we'd won! Although we lost 9–1, I'll also never forget the time Jermain Defoe ran us ragged. He was only a youngster, on loan at the Cherries, but you could tell he was special. Even our goal was an

Formed in 1875, the club has had three venues in its time, and now plays home games at Victoria Park, Winton, which was once a field on Joys Farm.

own-goal! There have also been some exciting FA Vase games here, plus that away trip to Aldershot Town in the Hants Senior Cup, when we were so close to pulling off an unlikely victory. We were founder members of the Wessex League in 1986 and have almost won it on two occasions, in 1991, when we finished third, and 1995, when we were runners-up. Our time may yet come, but in the meantime we'll keep going because we love the game.'

Bournemouth Divisional FA has been overseeing local league football since 1920. It runs four divisions and four cups (Saturday) and six divisions and five cups (Sunday). Its HQ is at Hurn Bridge, Christchurch.

There are grass pitches at Iford Lane Playing Fields, Kings Park, Strouden Park, Muscliff Park, Slades Farm (Talbot Village), Wallisdown Rec, Kinson Manor and Fernheath (in between East and West Howe), and artificial pitches at Littledown, Pelhams Park (Kinson) and Sir David English Sports Centre (East Way, off Castle Lane).

One of the more notable local footballers was Vladimir Chertkov, editor of the works of Leo Tolstoy, who was exiled from Russia in 1897 due to Tsarist censors. He ended up living in Tuckton and playing left-back for Tuckton FC. Another exile, Alexander Sirnis, played left-wing. Well, they couldn't have been right-sided, could they?

Cricket

Cricket is played at seven locations: Dean Park, Winton Rec, Kings Park, Littledown, Slades Farm (Talbot Village), Kinson Manor and Chapel Gate. Bournemouth Cricket Club is the largest and most successful club in Dorset and the only club within the county playing in an ECB (England and Wales Cricket Board) Premier League. Its home ground is at Chapel Gate. Dorset County Cricket Club based at Dean Park plays Minor Counties fixtures and takes part in the MCCA Knockout Trophy. They won the Minor Counties Championship twice, in 2000 and 2010, and the MCCA Knockout Trophy once, in 1988, since its inception in 1983.

Kings Park cricket ground.

The first cricket in Bournemouth appears to have been played around 1852 in today's Upper Gardens. County cricket (Hampshire and Dorset) was played at the Dean Park ground, which first hosted cricket in 1871. England's most famous cricketer W.G. Grace played here. Lionel Tennyson, grandson of the poet Tennyson, captained Hampshire from 1919 to 1933, regularly playing at Bournemouth. The highest First Class innings by a Hampshire player was achieved at Bournemouth, Richard Henry Moore scoring 316 versus Warwickshire in 1937. He attended Bournemouth School. In 1961 and 1973 Hampshire clinched the County Championship at Bournemouth, while a record crowd of over 7,000 was set for a Sunday League match in 1975. In 1978 Hampshire won the Sunday League at Dean Park in front of over 5500. Hampshire ceased playing at the 6,000-capacity ground in 1992, and it was taken over by Parley Cricket Club from 2016, and has been used by Bournemouth University.

Dr John Daniel Jones was minister at St Andrew's Church, Richmond Hill (1898–1937) A keen cricketer and Hampshire supporter, it is said he once announced 'Over!' rather than 'Amen!' at a service during Bournemouth Cricket Festival. Former Warwickshire player Sydney Santall (1873–1957) retired to Brockley Road, Ensbury Park, where he died, aged 83. He took over 1,200 wickets, including W.G. Grace seven times. Hampshire and England cricketer Phil Mead (1887–1958) died in Boscombe. He scored the most runs in the County Championship, scored 48,892 runs for Hampshire, and exceeded 1,000 runs every season, except his first when he only played one match!

One interesting variant was so-called sea cricket (cricket in the sea) captured on a Pathé film of 1949, when it was a 'new sport'. Girls can be seen frolicking in the water, while spectators watch from the pier.

Golf

There are golf courses at Solent Meads (Hengistbury Head), Meyrick Park and Queens Park. Meyrick Park's 18-hole championship course (5802 yards) dates to 1894 and was the first municipally planned golf links in the country, designed by Scottish course architect Thomas Dunn. Triple Open Champion Henry Cotton (1907–87) said, 'There is no finer hole than that of the 14th at Meyrick Park.' Queens Park (6132 yards) dates to 1905 and is 'A beautiful course with a deep sense of history and tradition' (Peter Alliss). The course was laid out by John Henry Taylor, four-times Open Champion.

Playgolf Bournemouth in Riverside Avenue has a two-tier, 40-bay premier driving range which is floodlit, so open late every night; an 18-hole course, straddling the Bournemouth–Christchurch border, with players crossing the Stour on a bridge between the 12th and 13th holes; a shorter par-3 course; and a 9-hole footgolf course (a cross between football and golf).

Bournemouth-born Georgia Hall is a professional golfer who plays on the Ladies European Tour and won the 2018 British Women's Open. She was a member of nearby Ferndown Golf Club, and set the current Ladies course record of 67 at the age of 11.

Bowls and Pétanque (French Boules)

There are 11 outdoor bowling venues: Seafield Gardens (Southbourne), Boscombe Cliff, Knyveton Gardens, Argyll Gardens, Meyrick Park, Winton Rec, Kings Park, Swanmore Gardens (Pokesdown), Redhill Park, Moordown Rec and Pelhams Park (Kinson).

The first bowling green in Bournemouth appears to have been laid down in Meyrick Park in 1894.

Bournemouth and District Bowling Association runs a Saturday Premier League of six sections, inaugurated in 1906, plus a Saturday Triples League of two sections. There is also an Evening Triples League of seven sections, with fixtures on a Tuesday. Ladies are catered for by the Bournemouth and District Women's Bowling Association, which runs a league of five divisions, inaugurated in 1933. A guidebook of 1979 states that several greens were 'Cumberland-turfed' – apparently the 'bee's knees' for bowling greens.

According to *Bournemouth: A Miscellany*, the town had the first indoor bowling green in the country, built on the site of the first Winter Gardens, after the original glass building was demolished in 1935. Today, Bournemouth Indoor Bowls Centre at Kings Park allegedly has one of the largest greens in

Europe and prides itself on being friendly and open to all. It offers regular sessions between October and April and ad hoc the rest of the year.

There is a six-lane tenpin bowling alley at Oasis Fun, Glenfern Road. Verity Crawley is a professional tenpin bowler from Bournemouth and the only British woman bowling on the pro tour in the USA. Opened in February 2017, there is also an active pétanque club and seven-lane floodlit 'terrain' at Muscliff Park.

Tennis, Squash and Racketball

There are tennis courts at Seafield Gardens (Southbourne), Shelley Park, Central Gardens, Knyveton Gardens, Meyrick Park, Winton Rec, Swanmore Gardens (Pokesdown), Moordown Rec, Victoria Park, Redhill Park and Pelhams Park (Kinson). The 'bubble' over Bournemouth Tennis Centre in the Central Gardens was officially opened in 1983 by Roger Taylor, three-times Wimbledon Men's Singles Semi-finalist. The 'bubble' was burst by vandals before and after the opening.

Bournemouth Tennis Centre in the Central Gardens.

Virginia Wade, the first-ever US Open Women's Singles Champion (1968) and Australian Open Singles Champion (1972), and most famously Wimbledon Ladies' Singles Champion in 1977, was born in Bournemouth in 1945 (her father was the vicar at Holy Trinity Church on Old Christchurch Road 1942–47). Later she attended Talbot Heath School. As an amateur, Wade won the first 'open' tennis competition (open to professionals and amateurs) – the British Hard Court Open – which was played at Bournemouth in 1968, marking the start of the 'open era'.

Bournemouth Squash Club is based at Chapel Gate. There are also courts at the West Hants Club and the Suncliff Hotel. Racketball can be played at both Chapel Gate and the West Hants Club.

Athletics

Athletics was officially first staged at Dean Park in 1871, although events probably occurred five years earlier. Bournemouth Athletics Club is based at Kings Park Athletics Centre, an impressive all-weather facility with a full-range of track and field equipment.

Kings Park Athletics Centre.

Cycling and BMX

Bournemouth Arrow Cycling Club was formed in 1927 and riders participate in many forms of cycling, including time trials, road and track racing, cyclo-cross and mountain biking. Members of Bournemouth Jubilee Wheelers, founded in 1935 (the year of George V's silver jubilee), participate in all aspects of cycling. The Tornado Road Cycling Club started in 2013, with members regularly riding in Sportives, charity rides, Audax and time trials. Bournemouth Velodrome is a public facility at Slades Farm, Ensbury Park (opened 2011), with a 250-m outdoor banked cycle track.

Bournemouth Cycling Centre, Slades Farm. (Copyright Mike Faherty.)

Bournemouth BMX Club has been based at Iford Lane Playing Fields since 1981. The only race track in Dorset, it has hosted regional and national events. The club is open to all ages and they have a bank of club bikes. Other tracks are at Poole Lane BMX (West Howe), with shared use of the skate park at Slades Farm (Ensbury Park) and a small unmaintained BMX track at Noyce Gardens (Townsend).

BMX track at Iford Lane Playing Fields.

Swimming and Water Polo

Bournemouth Spartans Winter Sea Swimming Club was formed in 1950 and has been holding a Christmas Day 'dip' since 1951, which currently raises funds for Macmillan Caring Locally. 'Swim Bournemouth' is a competitive indoor swimming team offering opportunities to swimmers of all ages, from six-year-olds to aspiring Olympic medallists. There are public swimming pools at Littledown Centre and Stokewood Leisure Centre, Charminster (opened 1930, it has a traditional feel), Queens Park and Pelhams Park. There used to be pools at Kinson Road (1969–2010), inside the BIC and at Pier Approach. The latter opened in 1937 (costing £80,000) on the site of the old saltwater baths, and for many years there were aqua shows here, plus sports such as water polo. They closed in 1984.

One of the earliest instances of water polo (or water 'hand-ball') was off Bournemouth Pier in 1876. The game, watched by a large crowd, lasted 15 minutes, until the ball burst. Today, Bournemouth Swimming and Water Polo Club is based at Stokewood Leisure Centre.

Shooting, Archery and Darts

A rifle range existed on land adjacent to Queens Park, certainly back in 1910. Bournemouth Small Bore, Rifle and Pistol Club was based here, but has now relocated to Chapel Gate. The once-fashionable sport of archery was enjoyed at Cranborne Gardens from 1862, the site later used for the Winter Gardens. The sport was occasionally revived, with meetings taking place in Dean Park. Today, Bournemouth Archery Club is based at Chapel Gate. The Professional Darts Corporation (PDC) Premier League has played rounds at the BIC, featuring most of the world's best players.

Rugby Union

Rugby Union has been played in Bournemouth since 1888, at Dean Park, Iford and Northbourne. The Rugby Section (of the Bournemouth Sports Club) was the only rugby club in Hampshire and Dorset to keep going throughout the war. In 1923 Bournemouth RFC combined with the Sports Club team and since 1989 has been based at Chapel Gate. Oakmeadians RFC play their home games at Meyrick Park.

Hockey

Bournemouth Hockey Club, Dorset's premier club, is based at Chapel Gate and is open to players of all ages and abilities. The annual Easter Festival has been extremely popular since 1937.

Baseball

Baseball was played at Meyrick Park during WWI. Artist Eustace Nash spent 'a busy hour' sketching the match and its spectators (of which there were 8,000-odd). US and Canadian teams played a charity match to boost Mayor Sir Merton Russell-Cotes' war fund; the US won 4–1.

Boxing and Wrestling

Freddie Mills, World Light-Heavyweight Boxing Champion (1948–50), was born at 7 Terrace Road, The Triangle. There is a blue plaque at nearby St Michael's School, which Mills attended, and a memorial to him in the Littledown Centre, which was originally unveiled in the Lower Gardens in 1979. When Mills was knocked out by American Joey Maxim to lose his title, he lost three teeth. Steven Bendall, World Boxing Union Middleweight Champion, lives in Bournemouth and runs Bendalls Boxing in Parkstone, Poole. Grapple-fans are catered for with Superslam wrestling matches taking place at the Pavilion Ballroom or the BIC.

Ice Skating and Roller Skating

There was once an ice skating rink in Westover Road (first opened in 1910, with a new £50,000 rink opening in 1930). Robin Cousins, Olympic Figure Skating Champion 1980, skated here as a 7-year-old while on holiday, and Bournemouth Stags ice hockey team competed between 1983 and 1988. Ice cabarets were held, as well as a summer 'Ice Revue'. In 1987 the ice rink melted, flooding neighbouring shops below. The rink closed in 1991. A temporary, but significant, 'real' ice rink is set up in the Lower Gardens for the Christmas period, and the BIC transforms the Purbeck Hall into the 'Cool Coast' ice rink between December and February.

The Mermaid Theatre opened on Boscombe Pier in 1962 to cater for the then-craze of roller skating, which also occurred on Bournemouth Pier (on a teak floor) and the Winter Gardens (from as early as 1876 on a cement surface). There is still roller skating today at the BIC, and a number of roller discos are in operation, such as at the Sir David English Sports Centre.

Some that Have Been and Gone

The gymkhana and fete in Meyrick Park in 1918 was attended by some 10,000 spectators. Proceeds aided the Bournemouth POW fund and New Zealand Wounded Soldiers Fund. In 1922, £1 shares went on sale to fund a £150,000 horse-race course at Ensbury Park, which opened in 1925, and staged races between the wars. By 1942 the race course was no more, with corn and spuds grown on the site, as Britain 'dug for victory'.

In a 1925–26 guide, public croquet lawns were listed at Argyll Gardens, Boscombe Cliff and Dean Park. Giant chess and draughts were popular on both piers right up to the 1980s, while you might have seen a game of quoits or shuffleboard on Bournemouth Pier in the 1930s.

The prestigious Schneider Trophy seaplane races were held at Bournemouth in 1919. The course was triangular, with the start and finish off Bournemouth Pier. An Italian team won in foggy conditions, but was later disqualified, so that competition was voided from the records. The end of WWI was marked by a 'victory show' of racing pigeons courtesy of the Bournemouth Premier Flying Club. Several of the birds had been on government service during the war. 'Mealy' was 'Best Old Bird in Show'.

Leisure Centres

'BH Live', a social enterprise and leading leisure and event operator, is responsible for managing three leisure centres in Bournemouth in partnership with the council: Littledown, Pelhams and Stokewood. It manages Sir David English in partnership with Bournemouth School Charitable Trust. It also manages leisure centres in Queens Park close to the town's leading municipal golf course, Corfe Mullen in Poole, and seven leisure, sporting and event venues in Portsmouth.

Littledown Centre is set in 47 acres of parkland and offers a 25-m pool, teaching pool, gym with over 200 'activity stations', artificial training pitches and an Altitude High Ropes Adventure attraction. Product Marketing Manager at BH Live Geoff Messenger has been at Littledown since it opened.

'Littledown's class timetable has more than 200 weekly group exercise classes, with kids and family fitness classes for 5- to 13-year olds (e.g. Family Yoga and Family Pilates) to encourage family participation, plus activities like Zumba, Aqua and Circuit Training. This has always been a family-oriented facility, borne out by our Under 5s Crèche and Soft Play area. We have something for everybody though, with the sports halls offering badminton, volleyball and basketball, plus the six artificial training pitches outside and cricket pitch and pavilion. Littledown is also home to sporting events including football tournaments, swimming galas and baton twirling competitions.

Littledown Centre opposite Bournemouth Hospital opened in March 1989.

As trends in fitness activities change, we have to change too, such as providing more floor space for small groups working out together and gym-based group exercise classes. Fitness is a big deal worldwide and we're proud that Bournemouth is one of the more active places in the UK and of the contribution Littledown and our other centres make to this. In fact, Littledown is one of the busiest leisure centres in Britain, with some 25,000–30,000 visits every week.

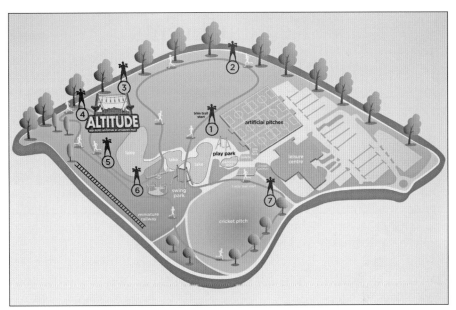

Littledown Centre and Park.

We have a healthy membership, which is now over 10,000 strong, but we also provide 'pay-as-you-go' and concessions for people on low income. As well as all the facilities we have on offer here, the park itself, winning a Green Flag Award in 2019, is actually a lovely place to relax and unwind too, with the attractive lake at its heart and it is a great setting for outdoor festivals and events.'

West Hants Club in Talbot Woods was founded in 1926. It is a members club, although new members are welcome. Following a major rebuild in 1999, the club offers internationally renowned clay tennis courts, an indoor tennis centre and a range of other facilities (squash courts, gym, two fitness studios, indoor heated pool and dedicated high-performance gym).

Regular Events

With over 500 events each year, Bournemouth is renowned for its busy calendar and is proud to be an eventful town. Here's a selection of the best.

April/May

In April **Bournemouth Bay Run** is a coastal half marathon, 10 km, 5 km or 1 km family fun run. **Bournemouth 7s** is a big deal on the last May Bank Holiday weekend. In 2018 over 30,000 people descended on the Bournemouth Sports Club facility, including 3,500 campers, with over 400 teams playing rugby, netball, hockey, volleyball and even dodgeball.

First staged in the late 1950s, **Pine Walk Art Exhibition** in the Lower Gardens has displays from May to September of painting, photography, sculpture, jewellery and digital art. Artists are on hand to discuss their work, which may be browsed and purchased.

One of the longest running art exhibitions in the country. (Copyright Bournemouth Borough Council.)

June/July

Bournemouth Food and Drink Festival takes place over 10 days in June. Based around The Square, the event includes a Street Food Festival and Demo Kitchen featuring some of the best local chefs.

Bournemouth Pride Festival 'Bourne Free', which first started in 2005, is an LGBT celebration of all diversities that live in Bournemouth. A different theme is chosen each year; for example, in 2017 it was 'Superheroes' and in 2018 'Hawaiian Beach Party'. One of the highlights is the parade, featuring colourful floats, music and dancing.

July/August

Shake & Stir Vintage Festival takes place in Southbourne, focused around Fisherman's Walk, Southbourne Grove and the Green. It features music, dancing, classic cars and a host of food and drink stalls.

Shake & Stir Vintage Festival. (Copyright Mandy Payne.)

Hundreds participate in the **Pier to Pier Swim**, which has raised over £220,000 for charity (2018), and 1,800 took part in 2017. Starting at Bournemouth Pier, hardy souls swim 1.4 miles to Boscombe Pier, raising money for the British Heart Foundation. Swimmers head off in two groups at 10 am and 11:40 am. The event was first staged in 1991.

Bournemouth Regatta generally occurs on a Saturday in July or August. Throughout most of the 20th century this was the seaside's principal event of the summer. The 1904 regatta featured rowing, sailing and swimming races, a lifeboat demo, water-polo match and shoreline sports, with a decorated boat competition for the children. Unfortunately support has declined of late.

Bournemouth Regatta. (Bournemouth Graphic. Courtesy of Bournemouth Libraries.)

The tradition of **lighting candles** in the Lower Gardens dates back to the visit of Empress Elizabeth of Austria in 1896, when a gardener provided a few candles to light the way as she walked to the beach. In 2017 this event was replaced by candlelit processions. Friday night **fireworks** take place in August from 10 pm, the display occurring from Bournemouth Pier.

In the past, 15,000 tea lights in glass holders, arranged in patterns such as a huge Union flag, have been lit using free tapers on Wednesday evenings. (Copyright Bournemouth Tourism.)

August/September

Bournemouth Air Festival takes place over 4 days around the end of August/beginning of September, and generally includes displays by the famous Red Arrows. The show commenced in 2008 and had entertained over 9 million people up to 2017, making it Europe's largest single-audience event. The festival site covers 1½ miles of Bournemouth's award-winning coastline.

Bournemouth Air Festival. (Copyright Bournemouth Tourism.)

October

Bournemouth Arts by the Sea Festival (launched 2012) includes over 60 events. The event features dance, film, music, visual art, literature, theatre and comedy, with some of the best regional, national and international artists. It utilises some of Bournemouth's best places and spaces, from the traditional to the unexpected.

Bournemouth Arts by the Sea Festival. (Copyright Bournemouth Tourism.)

Bournemouth Marathon Festival was launched in 2013 and has raised millions of pounds for charity. It includes eight distances with a full marathon, half-marathon, 10k and 5k races, plus junior events. It is somewhat unusual as there is guaranteed entry.

November/December

A service is held at Bournemouth War Memorial in the Central Gardens each **Remembrance Sunday**. There are parades of ex-servicemen and women and youth organisations.

Bournemouth Christmas Market takes place from mid-November to the first week of January. The previous German market theme was replaced by an Alpine market in 2017, offering boutique and local craft products and food stalls, focusing on local traders and suppliers. The centrepiece was a two-storey Alpine lodge, with Christmas-themed beverages. Bournemouth's **outdoor ice rink** operates in the Lower Gardens from mid-November until New Year. There is also the **Gardens Christmas Wonderland** featuring over a hundred trees lit with a million light bulbs.

Bournemouth Christmas Market. (Copyright Bournemouth Tourism.)

Macmillan White Christmas Dip takes place at 10:30 am on Christmas Day at Boscombe Pier and is a fundraising event for Macmillan Caring Locally. The event began in 2008 and involves charging into the sea at the appointed time. Over its first 9 years it raised over £130,000 for the Macmillan Unit in Christchurch Hospital; 960 swimmers took part in 2018.

Interesting Buildings and Businesses

This section is intended to capture some of Bournemouth's significant buildings that are perhaps not described fully or mentioned much elsewhere in the book.

Department Stores

Over the years, Bournemouth has had numerous department stores in and close to The Square. People may remember Bealesons, Plummer Roddis, J.J. Allen and Bobby's. In 1887, Kentish draper Frederick James Bobby started expanding his business, opening stores in specially selected towns, mostly seaside resorts. In 1915, a Bobby & Co.'s department store opened on the west side of The Square, in the curved building (today's Debenhams). It opened as a fashion store, which Bobby's was most famous for (celebrities would often visit the fashion showrooms). The store was severely bomb damaged in May 1943 but reopened after only a 9-week refit. In 1964, Harvey Nichols opened a furniture and carpet showroom on the third floor and the following year saw Bobby's celebrate its 50 years in some style. The successful company was later subsumed by Debenhams, and finally in 1972 the name of Bobby's disappeared.

Also, in the late 1800s, shopkeepers William Plummer, George Roddis and Reginald Tyrrell combined forces and grew a chain of department stores across southern England. Tyrrell branched off on his own, leaving the other two to run things. Plummer Roddis department store (1898) occupied the site at the junction of Old Christchurch Road and Gervis Place (Roddis House), and was later bought out by Debenhams in the late 1960s. This closed in 1973, but many of the staff moved across The Square to the new Debenhams (formerly Bobby & Co.).

J.J. Allen, house furnisher, carpet importer, cabinet maker, decorator, funeral furnisher and warehouseman, established his company around 1860. The business expanded into a chain of department stores. The first J.J. Allen store was on St Peter's Road, opposite the church. In 1960 the company bought out Bright's (see below), before being purchased itself by Dingles, which in turn became a division of House of Fraser. The Dingles name disappeared in 2006. The original Bright's store is used by House of Fraser, while the J.J. Allen store is now mostly occupied by T.K. Maxx and the Mary Shelley pub at the rear. One part of the original company, J.J. Allen Funeral Directors, remains a local business today, called Westbourne Funeralcare, and is part of the Co-op Funeralcare group.

In 1871, Fred Bright opened a needlework and wool store in Bournemouth Arcade. He soon expanded his business into books and printing, stationery and fancy goods and moved into larger premises at 14–26 Old Christchurch Road. Fred's son Percy took over the business in the 1920s. Percy was thrice Mayor of Bournemouth (1929–32). J.J. Allen bought the brand in 1960.

Of all the department stores Bournemouth has seen over the years, its flagship store is Beales, still occupying the original site where founder John Elmes Beale opened his first 'Fancy Fair and Oriental' store in 1881. An old part of the building on Gervis Place is dated 1887. He was the town's mayor from 1902 to 1904 and went on to expand his stores around the country. It is believed Bournemouth Beales was the first department store in Britain to have a real-life Father Christmas in 1885 and it was renowned for its Christmas parades through the town from 1885 until 1988. The 'Easter Farm' was another popular seasonal event, which began in 1913 and featured real animals. Beales is the only department store in Bournemouth still trading under its original name. The company was passed down through the family until Nigel Beale, the great-great-grandson of the founder, took over in the 1980s, and he is still Honorary President. Nigel says:

'I have seen Beales grow over the years, particularly when it acquired the Anglia Co-operative stores. At one time there were around 30 Beales stores, and we still have [around] 20 today, including Kendal, Bedford and Worthing, but Bournemouth was, of course, the first. I'm sure the business has grown beyond the wildest dreams of its founder.

At one time Bournemouth had more department stores than any other place of a corresponding size in Europe. People might also remember "Bealesons" (from Beale and sons), which was bought from a draper, Mr Okey, around 1920 (and traded until 1982). We had the curious situation of four Beale brothers effectively competing against one another (two at Beales and two at Bealesons). Although the Beales business was sold in 2015, it still retains a link with the family and I'm proud that we're still here and still trading under that name. We have a lot of loyal customers, with over 50,000 Beales loyalty card holders around the UK. Some of that loyalty went right back to WWII when we were bombed out. People wanted to see the store rebuilt and reopen. Over the years our customers have appreciated the stability that we offer; if something has gone wrong with a purchase, we've always been here the next day to sort it out. Personally, I always liked to work on a Saturday, meeting and greeting customers on the sales floor. Beales has always been about making friends as much as making sales, something our founder appreciated only too well.'

Railway Stations

For a town of its size, it is surprising that Bournemouth has only two stations, Bournemouth and Pokesdown. The 'Brief History' chapter provides details of other, lost stations. The coming of the railway certainly influenced the development of Westbourne. In July 1916, wounded soldiers from the Battle of the Somme arrived at the old Bournemouth West train station, on their way to Mont Dore military hospital. The aptly named *Pines Express* from Manchester operated between 1927 and 1962. WWII saw Bournemouth West receiving special non-stop trains from London, as nearby Poole Harbour had become the only place where civilians could fly in and out of the country (courtesy of Imperial Airways flying boats).

Bournemouth Central Station is part of a travel interchange slightly over a mile from the beach. Built in 1885, it was likened to a 'winter gardens' by author

Bournemouth railway station.

Lawrence Popplewell and it is easy to see why, with its train-shed roof a myriad of glass panes. We're lucky to still have it, as it was badly damaged in the great storm of 1987, after which a total rebuild was considered. The venerable train-shed was saved courtesy of a multi-million-pound investment by Railtrack (2000). One thing you won't see today is a real live dog with a collecting box strapped to its back. These animals once collected for the London and South Western Railway Servants' Orphanage and were a fixture at the central station ('Bournemouth Nell' and 'Bournemouth Bob', for example).

Pokesdown Station opened in July 1886 after a lengthy campaign by Pokesdown and Boscombe residents, as the main Bournemouth Station was perceived to be too distant. Pokesdown was in a deep cutting, however, so not ideally placed, with a long flight of steps leading down to the island platform, which had tracks either side. The station is estimated to have cost around £2,000. Boscombe would get its own station in 1897 (to 1965). Pokesdown meanwhile was extensively rebuilt in 1930/31, when the line was quadrupled and the island platform replaced with two new side platforms. A new bridge connected them and a new station entrance was also created in Christchurch Road. During the 1970s the two centre tracks were removed, which makes the platforms seem very far apart today.

Pokesdown station.

Churches

Bournemouth has three Grade I Listed churches: St Peter's and St Stephen's in the town centre (see Walk 1) and St Clement's in Boscombe. St Peter's in Hinton Road was Bournemouth's first church, under the inaugural vicar Rev. Alexander Morden Bennett. The first church on this site was consecrated in 1845, but the church we see today really began in 1853 when Morden Bennett commissioned George Edmund Street to design a new St Peter's, which became one of England's finest Victorian buildings. The tower was finished in 1870 and the 202-ft spire added in 1879, which effectively completed the church, shortly before the passing of Morden Bennett. Foremost craftsmen were employed throughout, for example, Sir Ninian Comper, who also designed the separate Chapel of the Resurrection as a war memorial and mortuary chapel in 1925/26. St Peter's prides itself on being 'a warm, lively and inclusive church in the open and liberal catholic tradition of the Church of England. We cherish education, music and literature.'

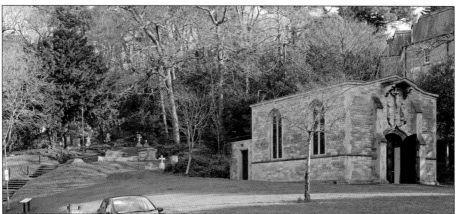

St Peter's Church.

The current rector is Rev. Ian Terry.

'I have been here since 2009. As town centre rector I minister not only at St Peter's, but also St Stephen's (built as a memorial to our founder Morden Bennett) and St Augustine's. St Peter's is my main church, however, and I spend most time here. Our mission statement is to work with other bodies to help this place [Bournemouth] and its community thrive. We see the church as a 'safe haven', used by people of all ages, as well as being a place of peace and rest, and somewhere fascinating to be

looked around. We aim to be active within the community, for example, with our "nightclub chaplaincy", volunteers who will help people in need, "guardian angels" if you like, who will help when people might become vulnerable on a night out. We also have a tradition of engaging with rough sleepers, advertising where they can find free food and drink and where they can "sleep safe". On Tuesdays we now have "Music for Dementia Sufferers"; it's recognised now how reminiscing can re-energise people. We're excited about our "Stone and Voice" project, which will research the 24 fallen soldiers whose names are in the mortuary chapel. The aim is to bring their stories alive, and, in the process, share the story of this remarkable chapel. One of our best-kept secrets is the Shelley tomb, where Frankenstein authoress Mary Shelley lies, along with her radical parents. We also want to make more of this as we celebrate the wonderful diversity that Bournemouth has. When the Bournemouth Air Festival takes place, we'll have an open air service at the bandstand in Pine Walk, as we seek to be a part of these major local events. This is another example of St Peter's wanting to be very much at the heart of the community that it serves.'

St Stephen's in St Stephen's Way was constructed in stages from 1881 by John Loughborough Pearson, a Gothic Revival architect noted for his work on cathedrals and churches. His aim with St Stephen's was to 'bring people to their knees'. It is often dubbed the Bennett Memorial Church as it was built to commemorate the Reverend. The style is Early English, the nave spacious and impressive, with lovely screens and reredos, and stained glass by Clayton and Bell.

St Clement's (1871) in St Clement's Road, Boscombe, was the first major church designed by architect John Dando

St Stephen's Church.

Sedding, with the tower added later after Sedding's death. It is hard to imagine now, but early vicars were subject to 'stonings' from irate crowds purely because of the type of service (based on the Oxford Movement, which was Anglo-Catholic, so offensive to some). The chancel is dominated by a huge reredos of G.W. Seale,

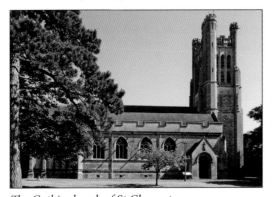

The Gothic church of St Clement.

while there are two remarkable south windows by Christopher Whall. Next to the church was the Sisters of Bethany orphanage (1875–1939), which provided a home for over 100 children in some 6 acres of grounds. Some of this is used as offices today, with the rest demolished for housing. The founder, Etheldreda Anna Bennett lies buried in the churchyard.

The town's largest church is Richmond Hill St Andrew's United Reformed Church, built in 1865 and enlarged in 1891. St Andrew's has a seating capacity of nearly 1100, with unusual curved pews that help create a cosy, informal atmosphere. It has been claimed to be the 'most beautiful Nonconformist Church in England'. It is lofty like a cathedral and has magnificent stained-glass windows, whereas Nonconformist churches were normally more austere, eschewing much or any adornment.

St Andrew's United Reformed Church.

In 1869 Holy Trinity Church was built in Old Christchurch Road, facing the entrance to Glen Fern Road. It was an unusual-looking church, in Romanesque style, with a distinctive, tall, brick-built tower a later addition, which gave it its nickname the 'Rocket Church'. TB patients were once allowed to worship here, enclosed by a glass screen in a designated area. The church burnt down in 1981 and the site is now occupied by offices of the *Bournemouth Echo*.

Holy Trinity Church, showing the 'new' tower in 1957. (Courtesy of Bournemouth Libraries.)

Hotels

There are hotels, of course, too numerous to mention, and catering for every taste and pocket. Many are mentioned in the Walks later in this book.

Tregonwell's 'first house' is today the Royal Exeter Hotel in Exeter Road (named after the Marchioness).

The Royal Exeter Hotel did not start life as a hotel. Between 1810 and 1812 it was built as The Mansion, a home for Lewis Tregonwell. However, he did not always reside in Bournemouth, and in 1820 it was let to the Marchioness of Exeter. It was used as a private boys' school (Exeter House Collegiate School) between 1858 and 1876. Then it became Exeter House Hotel, and later Newlyn's Royal and Imperial Hotel, hosting distinguished visitors including the Empress Elizabeth of Austria and her daughter the Archduchess Marie Valerie in 1888.

The oldest existing hotel in Bournemouth is the Royal Bath on Bath Road. It was opened on the same day as Queen Victoria's Coronation, 28 June 1838. Merton Russell-Cotes bought it in 1876 as a going concern, but also to display his many art treasures, and renamed it the Royal Bath. Many famous people have stayed there, including D.H. Lawrence, Sir Richard Branson, Sting, Kevin Keegan and Oscar Wilde. In 2012, while filming the TV series

In 1979 the Royal Bath's east wing (around one-third of the hotel) was consumed by fire, Bournemouth's biggest hotel blaze since WWII, yet by 1990 it was the country's top hotel according to the AA, with a 5-star rating.

Great British Railway Journeys, Michael Portillo (who describes himself as a 'former-future prime minister') was given a room here and was delighted to discover he was in good company: PM Benjamin Disraeli held three Cabinet Councils here in the winter of 1874/75, while Lord John Russell, Gladstone, Asquith and Lloyd George also stayed here (the Gladstone Bar and Oscar's Brasserie recall just two of the famous people who've stayed). During WWII officers of the Royal Canadian Air Force were billeted here. Also built around 1838 was the Belle Vue Boarding House, which stood where the Pavilion is now and later became the Belle Vue and Pier Hotel.

The Carlton was built originally as a private house on the East Cliff in 1861 and converted to a hotel in 1903. An electrically operated lift to all floors was installed in 1911 and by 1934 the hotel was granted 5-star rating (for many years it was the only privately owned 5-star hotel in Europe). In 1944 Generals Eisenhower and Montgomery stayed here while watching D-Day rehearsals in the bay. At the end of the war the hotel was a temporary home for GI brides, awaiting the return of their beaux from Europe. Among politicians to have stayed are Harold Macmillan, Enoch Powell, 'Rab' Butler and PM Anthony Eden, who stayed in 1955 during the Conservative conference. Entertainers Eartha Kitt, Gracie Fields, Anna Neagle, Sid James and Morecambe and Wise have also stayed, plus playwright Terence Rattigan and tennis player Virginia Wade. According to an old advert for the Carlton, it offered the 'finest position on the East Cliff, facing full south, with a beautiful Marine Sun Lounge, sheltered from North and East, with a private garage for six cars'.

The Hotel Miramar on the East Cliff is notable for its association with J.R.R. Tolkien. The ground floor has several items of memorabilia, including a large map of 'Middle Earth' signed by Tolkien, a framed luncheon menu, which he also signed, and a photograph of the author relaxing on the terrace, with trademark pipe.

The Hotel Miramar.

Brompton Court

Back in 1855, the Medical Committee of the Royal Brompton Hospital decided to build a small sanatorium in Bournemouth. Thus the Royal National Sanatorium for Consumption and Diseases of the Chest was founded, the first of its kind anywhere in the world. It comprised 97 beds and was almost entirely supported by voluntary contributors. The building was extended in 1863 by Christopher Crabb Creeke and included a chapel. In 1974 it became an NHS hospital, which then

Brompton Court. (Courtesy of the Kingsdale Group.)

closed in the late 1980s. In 2000 Bovis Homes converted it into Brompton Court, and it is now run by Kingsdale Property Management Group offering very desirable assisted living apartments and bungalows.

Town Hall

Bournemouth has had not one but four town halls over the years (see Walk 1). The current Town Hall on Bourne Avenue is housed in a beautiful Italianate building. Thomas Beach's portrait of Bournemouth's founder Lewis Tregonwell hangs inside the hall. On the site originally was a villa called the Glen, a boarding house which was demolished in 1881 to make way for a magnificent hotel, the Mont Dore. This was one of a number of 'hydropathic hotels' that sprang up in town, offering a luxurious 4-acre spa, where the 'Mont Dore Cure' (from the Auvergne spa town of Mont Dore) was proffered by Dr Horace Dobell, primarily to rich consumptives.

The Mont Dore consisted of five storeys, with two areas under one roof. First, the spa, comprising vapour douches and baths, inhalation halls, nasal and throat irrigations, hot and cold plunge pools, needle, pine, electric and other baths, and a luxurious Turkish bath. The various baths used fresh water from the Bourne or salt water pumped from the sea. The facility was well situated next to the Royal National Sanatorium. The second part of the hotel consisted of 120 bed and sitting rooms, a grand dining room, ladies

Bournemouth Town Hall, with its steep, château-style roof reminiscent of its French (Mont Dore) connections.

drawing room, reading, billiard and smoking rooms, music and ball room, and winter garden affording sheltered nooks. During WWI the building was commandeered as a convalescent home for wounded officers and later as a military hospital. In 1921 it became the town hall.

The Pavilion

Purpose-built as an entertainment complex in 1928/9 with a theatre seating 1,500, a ballroom and supper rooms, the Pavilion was one of the most modern theatres in the country in the 1930s. It occupies the site of one of Bournemouth's oldest buildings, the Belle Vue Hotel, which included Mr Sydenham's early library and reading rooms. Many performers have appeared here, including David Bowie in 1965, in his previous guise as 'Davie Jones and the Lower Third' (he reinvented himself because of potential confusion with The Monkees' Davy Jones). It has a revolving stage and the orchestra pit is on a lift so it can be

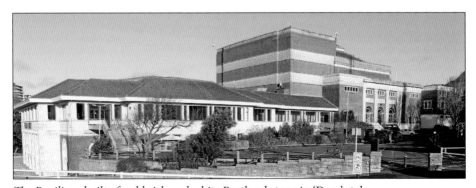

The Pavilion, built of red brick and white Portland stone in 'Deco' style.

raised when the band strikes up the overture. In June 2019, the Pavilion hosted the Conservative party's third leadership hustings, with Jeremy Hunt and Boris Johnson fielding questions from local party members.

The Opera House, Boscombe (now the O2 Academy Bournemouth)

The Victorian terraced building at 568–578 Christchurch Road began life in the late 1880s as the Arcade Pavilion, as a theatre, hotel, billiard hall and shopping arcade. Not everyone was happy having a theatre here as it was considered bawdy and improper in those days. Over the years, it had various uses (including as a circus) and several name changes. A new building was opened in 1895 as the Grand Theatre and Pavilion at a cost of £15,000. It became Boscombe Grand Theatre in 1899 and Boscombe Hippodrome some years later. From 1945 it was owned by a local family, the Butterworths, who ran 17 other theatres. It continued to be popular until 1957, when theatre began to lose out to television,

Grade II Listed Boscombe Grand Theatre.

and it was converted into a dance hall, the Royal Ballrooms. This continued until 1972, when it became a disco and nightclub (Tiffany's). In 1982, the name changed again to the Academy, which won Best UK Club several times in the mid-1980s, before becoming the Academy 2 and then, in 1997, the Opera House, when big acts such as Frankie Goes to Hollywood and the Sisters of Mercy performed here. In 2006 it had a £3.5m refurbishment for use as a 'general venue' in the style of its theatre origins, recreating the ornate Victorian plasterwork, restoring and reopening the 'Gods' area, and installing specialist LED lighting. It is now the O2 Academy Bournemouth.

Russell-Cotes House, Gallery and Garden

The simple fact we have a museum in Bournemouth today is easily taken for granted. It is the legacy of the town's mayor and local philanthropist Sir Merton and his wife Lady Annie Russell-Cotes. They were great travellers and collectors, who donated their house (formerly East Cliff Hall) along with its eclectic treasures to the town in 1907, via a 'living will', enabling the couple to stay in the house until they died. The gift also celebrated the opening of the first part of the town's Undercliff (from the Pier to Meyrick Road), of which Sir Merton was a great supporter.

Sir Merton had the house on East Cliff Promenade built between 1897 and 1901 as an extravagant birthday present for his wife, and it is a fine example of the grandeur of the late Victorian era. In September 2001, following a £3 million renovation, Prince Richard, Duke of Gloucester and first cousin to the Queen, reopened the Gallery and Museum. The current curator is Duncan Walker.

'I've been at the Russell-Cotes since 2007, and curator since 2015. I have a very broad remit, which includes acquisitions and disposals, collating what we have (and making sure we know where it all is!) and reconciling this with what the accession registers say we should have, giving talks and lectures, income generation, for example from image licencing, "collections care", which includes pest management (moths, beetles, etc.), answering enquiries, loaning out items, participating in the exhibitions programme and so on. With around 45,000 items, we can sustain a rolling programme of exhibitions very largely from our own collection, bearing in mind that only a small proportion of the total (around 2%) is ever on show.

We owe a massive debt to the Russell-Cotes, of course, who gave the people of Bournemouth this house and its contents. They were avid collectors and Sir Merton was still acquiring pieces right up to the end. For me, he was a fascinating man, full of contradiction, yet also very much a man of his time. He

refused to let his son Herbert pursue a career on the stage, yet we have the Irving Collection here, he raged against the modern world, yet benefited from it, argued against votes for women, yet acquired a collection of female artists. There was a commercial purpose to his collecting as he used his collection as a "draw" to the Royal Bath Hotel, which he had purchased in 1876; all part of his master-plan for making this end of town the lynchpin of Bournemouth. Even though he was our Mayor and a philanthropist, he attracted criticism as there was a suspicion that every decision was geared towards maintaining the Royal Bath and the East Cliff in its pre-eminent position. Whatever we may think of Merton, his act of generosity was amazing and has inspired people to generously give to the collections ever since. Of our 900 odd oil paintings, most of them originated with him. What's also nice is that the Russell-Cotes' story appears to have been a genuine love match. They were both born in 1835 and appear to have been equal partners, deriving equal pleasure from their travel and collecting. We now have to take a leaf out of Merton's book and work hard to keep the museum in the public eye.'

Other Interesting Buildings

Bournemouth Natural Science Society

Bournemouth Natural Science Society (BNSS) was formed in 1903 with the aim of promoting the study of all branches of science and natural history. It has been exhibiting its collections in its current home, a Grade II Listed, late-Victorian building at No. 39 Christchurch Road, since 1919. These

collections, which have been mostly donated by members, include animals, birds, insects and plants; archaeology; astronomy; Egyptology; geography and geology; science; and the garden. In 2016, the BNSS was awarded Accredited Museum status by the Arts Council England. The collections may be viewed on Tuesdays between 10am and 4pm.

(Courtesy of BNSS.)

The Knole Freemasons' Hall (Walk 5 map)

Today's Tudor-style Freemasons' Hall (formerly The Knole) in Knole Road was built in 1873 for philanthropic and wealthy bachelor Edmund Christy, by renowned architect John Dando Sedding. It later became the home of Sir Henry Page Croft, Bournemouth's first MP.

Boxer Rocket Shed (Walk 6 map)

The little 'Boxer Rocket Shed' in Dalmeny Road (opposite Wildown Road) in Southbourne was used by the nearby Coastguard to store their Boxer rockets, which fired rescue lines to ships in distress.

Lansdowne College (Walk 2)

Bournemouth & Poole College at the Lansdowne is housed in an impressive Edwardian Baroque-style building. Building work started in 1910 and it opened in 1913 as the Municipal College with 780 students. A wing housed the town's first central library, only the second in Britain operating under the open-access system. The building's landmark clock tower was dubbed Mate's Folly, after Charles Mate (Chair of the Education Committee), as the clock has no numbers.

Original 1952 Listed Domestic Buildings

(From 'Streets of Bournemouth' online pdf)

Listed domestic buildings 1952	Date of building
Manor Farmhouse, Manor Farm Lane, Kinson	About 1700
17, Old House, Holdenhurst	17th century
Littledown House, Holdenhurst Road	1780
16, New House, Holdenhurst	Late 17th century
228 Broadway Lane (The Shack)	Late 17th century
Muscliff House (Farmhouse), Muscliffe Lane	Late 18th century
Stour View Cottage, Throop Road	About 1790
90, Wick Farmhouse, Wick Lane	Not known
Holdenhurst Farmhouse	Not known, demolished 1965
Throop House, Throop Road	About 1800
78–84, Wick House, Wick Lane	About 1800
Royal Exeter Hotel, Exeter Road	1810–12
The Thatched House, East Howe Lane	1820
38 Richmond Hill (Constitutional Club)	1838

Interestingly, most of these buildings are in the outlying villages that were later incorporated into Bournemouth. Only the Royal Exeter Hotel and 38 Richmond Hill from the original settlement of Bourne were considered suitable for inclusion. In addition to the above domestic buildings, several churches including St Peter's, St John's (Holdenhurst), St Andrew's (Kinson), St Michael's, St Clement's (Boscombe) and St Stephen's were listed, as were Iford and Longham Bridges.

Architects

Many architects have played a key role in designing Bournemouth and its buildings, including Benjamin Ferrey and Christopher Crabb Creeke. There is also a notable Bournemouth-born architect whose claim to fame lies elsewhere. Elisabeth Scott (1898–1972) was born in the town and attended Redmoor School, Canford Cliffs, Poole. She was related to the famous Gilbert Scott architects, becoming an architect herself, who went on to design the Shakespeare Memorial Theatre in Stratford-upon-Avon (opened 1932), the first significant public building designed by a female architect in the UK.

Exploring

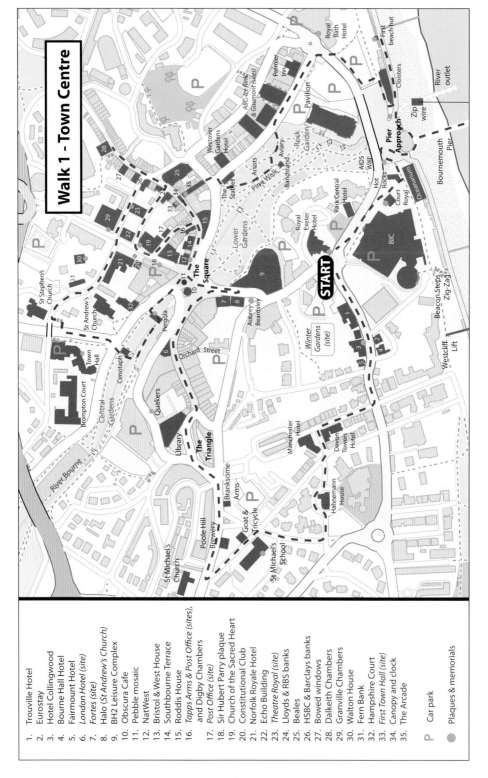

Walk 1 - Town Centre

1. Trouville Hotel
2. Eurostay
3. Hotel Collingwood
4. Bourne Hall Hotel
5. Fairmount Hotel
6. *London Hotel (site)*
7. *Fortes (site)*
8. Halo (*St Andrew's Church*)
9. BH2 Leisure Complex
10. Obscura Cafe
11. Pebble mosaic
12. NatWest
13. Bristol & West House
14. Southbourne Terrace
15. Roddis House
16. *Tapps Arms & Post Office (sites),* and Digby Chambers
17. *Post Office (site)*
18. Sir Hubert Parry plaque
19. Church of the Sacred Heart
20. Constitutional Club
21. Norfolk Royale Hotel
22. Echo Building
23. *Theatre Royal (site)*
24. Lloyds & RBS banks
25. Beales
26. HSBC & Barclays banks
27. Bowed windows
28. Dalkeith Chambers
29. Granville Chambers
30. Walton House
31. Fern Bank
32. Hampshire Court
33. *First Town Hall (site)*
34. Canopy and clock
35. The Arcade

P Car park
● Plaques & memorials

Walk 1: Town Centre

Start and finish:
Front of Royal Exeter Hotel
Approx. distance: 6 km

An apt starting point is the **Royal Exeter Hotel** as the plaque on the front wall commemorates Lewis Tregonwell building Bournemouth's first house here.

Cross over to Priory Road. The area to your right was once occupied by the **Winter Gardens**, but after many years as an ad-hoc car park it is now making way for an upmarket development by Bournemouth Development Company. Ascend the hill to **Trouville Hotel** (originally St Margaret's villa). This was bought by celebrated composer Dan Godfrey in 1903, but he vacated after WWI and by the 1920s it had become the Trouville boarding house. In 1932 it was combined with Garthlands Hotel.

Beyond Beacon Road, **Eurostay Bournemouth Beach** was previously West Cliff Towers Hotel in the 1880s. Today's student hotel has probably the largest collection of music memorabilia on the south coast (hence one of its previous names, Bourne Beat Hotel). **Bourne Hall Hotel** next door was previously West Cliff Hall Hotel, also built in the 1880s.

Dan Godfrey moved into No. 11 (Rosstrevor) between 1922 and 1934, which was built as a semi with 11a in 1874. This site is now occupied by **Hotel Collingwood**. A **blue plaque** here commemorates Godfrey's achievements. **Fairmount Hotel** was built in 1876 and still trades under its original name.

Turn second right into **St Michael's Road**, which once hosted a myriad of small boarding houses. **Devon Towers Hotel** is sizeable, but **Manchester Ho-**

tel is the biggest of the remaining hotels in this road and with over 100 rooms is Bournemouth's largest independent hotel. It regularly attracted celebrity entertainers, including Jim Davidson, Hattie Jacques and Tony Blackburn, who all entered its annual in-house 'star search' competition before making it big.

Just before the Manchester, turn left into Hahnemann Road, then cross West Hill Road, heading for the red-brick building straight ahead. **Hahnemann House**, which occupies the central 'island', was opened in June 1879 by Earl Cairns, Lord Chancellor, as Hahnemann Convalescent Home and Homeopathic

Dispensary. The house was for consumptive patients of modest means in the early stages of the condition who had a reasonable hope of recovery. Named after homeopathic pioneer Samuel Hahnemann, it doubled in size in 1884 and lasted until 1948 when it became part of the early NHS. It operates today as a convalescent home. Some old photos show building-wide cast-iron balconies on the south side.

Bear right around the island to exit Hahnemann Road into Durley Road (right). Note the big **deckchair** (left), in case you fancy a rest! Follow Durley Road right to the crossroads, passing **St Michael's School**, which was attended by World Light Heavyweight Boxing champion Freddie Mills. There is a **blue plaque** on the front of the school in Somerville Road.

Bear left into West Hill Road, passing the back of the school. On the right, the **Goat & Tricycle** has been voted 'best cask beer pub' in the country (2008).

When you reach Poole Hill, the church opposite is **St Michael's** (which gives its name to the local school and road you have walked down). It is an example of English Gothic architecture, the first part of which was consecrated in 1876.

Turn right down Poole Hill into Commercial Road. There is more brewery interest here. **Poole Hill Brewery** is a Victorian-inspired taproom offering

Southbourne Ales and Tingay's brands. The 20-barrel brewhouse is capable of producing 15,000 pints a week. It offers brewery tours and even has a small cinema.

Next door to the right is a little building with **AD 1882** on the gable. Over the years it has been occupied by a tailor and furrier, architect, fruiterer and florist, circulating library, social club, government surplus clothing store and hairdresser, and is currently a Vintage Tea Rooms.

Yeahman (Caribbean Kitchen) further down occupies a former public convenience on the centre island of Commercial Road.

The former **Branksome Arms**, a brewhouse and microbrewery, was built in 1905 in the style of Art Nouveau crossed with Edwardian Baroque, with the façade an exuberant combination of green-glazed brick with grey Carter's ceramic marble dressing.

Follow the road down, crossing at the lights to head left into The Triangle. The **Central Library** opened here in 2002 and **The Triangle** has become a vibrant and quirky hub for dining, live music, the arts, culture and night life. It has several ethnic restaurants, a real ale pub, daytime café culture, plus a lively nightlife with a selection of bars and clubs. Bournemouth has a well-established gay scene and most venues are based in The Triangle area. It also has several of the finest makeup studios in the region.

Bear right past the front of the library, then left into pedestrianised Commercial Road. You will pass **Orchard Street** (halfway down on the right). It is speculated that the word 'street' had working-class connotations, so it was only used in one place in Bournemouth (here) where working-class housing was sprouting up for those serving the genteel souls residing elsewhere in the town. We can explain the 'orchard' part as there was an orchard at the back of Commercial Road, which survived until 1851.

The last building on the left, **1 Commercial Road**, was the site of **London Hotel**, one of Bournemouth's three oldest hotels (the others being the Royal Bath and Belle Vue). The hotel was demolished in 1930, the site being rebuilt and occupied by John Collier clothing retailer, which was later bought out by Burtons.

Follow the pedestrianised area into **The Square**. This was the first crossing point over the Bourne stream, a bridge being built in 1849. It became known as The Square from 1858 (although why remains a mystery) and was pedestrianised in 2000.

Bear right off The Square into Exeter Road. Wetherspoon's The Moon in the Square pub is on the site of a landmark **Fortes** restaurant (1937), which sold Bournemouth's first cappuccino but burned down in 1993.

Next on the right, the **former Presbyterian church of St Andrew** is now rather incongruously a nightclub, aptly named **Halo**. Its spire was removed in 1947 after wartime bombing. Opposite is the site of the Central Bus and Coach Station, which operated from 1931 until it burned down in 1976. It is now dominated by the **BH2 Leisure Complex** (Odeon, etc.).

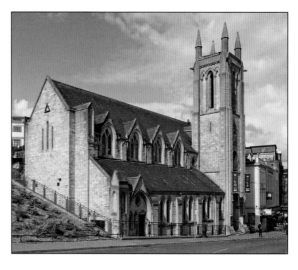

Just beyond the church, take the opportunity to admire the mosaic representing an **Aubrey Beardsley** design and view the plaque commemorating the artist.

Double-back into The Square to the **Obscura Café**. The clock on the roof was once atop the tram shelter here (1924–47).

Head across the **pebble fish mosaic** paving (by Maggy Howarth, 2009) towards **the foot of Richmond Hill** (previously Nurse or Nurses' Hill). In 1857 this was the site of the town's first Presbyterian church – the so-called Iron Scotch Church, as it was built originally of galvanised, corrugated iron. In 1872 it was replaced by a stone church; when this became too small, a new church was built in Exeter Road (now Halo). Next the site was occupied by Central Chambers (1888). This comprised the Mansion Hotel above (which became known as the Empress in 1906) and businesses below, including a Cadena café. In 1930, the next-door National Provincial Bank extended its premises, taking over the Cadena. The bank later became known as **NatWest** and still occupies the premises today. The Empress closed in 1953. A **blue plaque** on NatWest commemorates the site's rich history.

The equally grand Central Hotel occupied the next block up Richmond Hill on the right. Built in 1886, it offered 'special attention to commercial

gentlemen'. On 23 May 1943, the hotel took a direct hit by a German bomber, one of 12 attacks mounted that day. The blast killed 27 people (mostly airmen who had arrived the previous day). The hotel was too badly damaged to be repaired and was demolished. **Bristol & West** Building Society opened premises on the site in 1953 and the building we see today is a fine example of post-war Deco-inspired 'Moderne' architecture, with its curved corner tower.

To the right of NatWest, heading up Old Christchurch Road, you first pass **Southbourne Terrace**, built in 1865 as six shops with three storeys of domestic accommodation above. Three of these old shops were amalgamated as a WH Smith/post office. The road alongside the Lower Gardens, opposite, where the buses stop (Gervis Place), would once have had lines of charabancs rather than today's buses.

Roddis House ahead with its Deco-Moderne octagonal tower, used to be a Plummer Roddis department store. Today it is offices with shops below. Continue up Old Christchurch Road, then bear left into **Post Office Road**. Originally, the Tapps Arms (1809), and later Tregonwell Arms (1839), was at the start of this road on the left, with the front entrance of the pub

in Old Christchurch Road. The town's first post office used to be here too, with mail sorted on the old bar! The pub was demolished in 1885 and the post office moved up the road a little to the warm-coloured stone building on the right (now Pizza Express).

Digby Chambers (on the left as you enter Post Office Road), once the Digby Institute, was designed and built as a YWCA, where over a hundred girls were cared for under Miss Wingfield Digby. Attached was Havergal Hall, a room capable of seating 160 and used for public meetings and lectures.

At the end of this road you are back at Richmond Hill. Across to your left (next to the NCP) is a **blue plaque** commemorating the birthplace here of famous composer Sir Hubert Parry (famous for the tune of *Jerusalem*).

Head right up Richmond Hill and on the left is a two-storey white building (**No. 38**), the only surviving villa of central Bournemouth's earliest years. It was originally built in 1838 by architect Mr Shepherd for the Gordon estate, as one of three pairs of semi-detached villas, but was reduced to the one villa in 1930. It serves as the Bournemouth & District Constitutional Club, which began in Verulam Place, off Yelverton Road.

Next is the pink **Norfolk Royale Hotel**. It was originally built as two villas by the Tapps and converted to Stewart's Hotel in 1870. The cast-iron Art Nouveau

veranda was added in 1903. The 15th Duke of Norfolk was a regular visitor, hence its renaming in 1910. Curiously, it was the only fully licensed hotel not requisitioned during WWII. A **blue plaque** was unveiled by the 17th Duke of Norfolk after extensive refurbishment in 1988.

Another **blue plaque** in this road can be found at the base of the tower of the **Catholic Church of the Sacred Heart**, commemorating author and philanthropist Lady Georgiana Fullerton (1812–85), who worshipped here.

Contentious even today, Edgar Allan Poe wrote of her novel *Ellen Middleton*, 'A remarkable work, and one which I find much difficulty in admitting to be the composition of a woman … Not that many good and glorious things have not been the composition of women – but, because, here, the severe precision of style, the thoroughness, and the luminousness, are points never observable, in even the

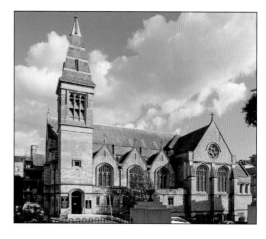

most admirable of their writings'. The insides of the church are well worth a visit, with some inspiring paintings and beautiful carved altar pieces.

Across Albert Road from the church is the Art Deco **Bournemouth Echo** building. Proceed down Albert Road, past **No. 16**, the Grade II listed former **Theatre Royal**,

which cost a massive £10,000 to construct in 1882 and seated 800. Five years later, strangely it was turned into the Town Hall, but reverted to a theatre in 1892; then in the 1960s it became a cinema, before being used as a night club, comedy club Twisters, and now a casino, with the old circle used as the venue's restaurant. .

Towards the end of Albert Road there used to be more *Echo* offices. **Lloyds** bank on the right corner was built around 1875 in classic Italian Baroque style, and is

somewhat matched by the ornate building opposite (**RBS** bank). Across Old Christchurch Road is the late Deco-inspired Moderne eight-storey **Beales** store. The roof hosted an anti-aircraft gunner during WWII. Don't miss the **pavement artwork and quotes** here, which were installed in 2019

Walk left up the road. There is an imposing white stone building on each corner of Yelverton Road, respectively **HSBC** (previously Midland, Bournemouth's oldest bank (1850)) and **Barclays** (1859).

On up the pedestrian street you pass the first-floor bowed glass windows of **71–73 Old Christchurch Road**, built in 1927, which would once have seen diners enjoying morning coffee, luncheons and afternoon teas, as this was another **Cadena Cafe** (the name comes from the special blend of 'cadena' coffee they used.) The building was also a Dillons bookstore in the 1990s.

Continue on to admire Grade II Listed Dalkeith Buildings on the left. Called **Dalkeith Chambers** today, it had been the home of Henry Laidlaw, who hailed from Dalkeith (Scotland) and established a horse-drawn omnibus service in Bournemouth in 1881. The building became Dalkeith Hotel in 1901. Richmond Gardens Arcade is now on the ground floor of the building but was previously the Dalkeith Arcade which opened in 1981.

Turn around and retrace your steps for approx. 50 m, then turn right into Yelverton Road. Up on the left is Genting Casino, with its **blue plaque** on what was the rear of the Theatre Royal.

At the end of Yelverton Road you are back at Richmond Hill again and the *Echo* offices are on your left. There are plans for the part-Grade II listed building to be redeveloped, including a three-storey glass extension on the roof.

On the right is **Granville Chambers**, built in 1885 as a temperance hotel and named after physician Dr Augustus Granville, whose recommendation of Bournemouth in his book *The Spas of England* (1841) helped put the town on the map. The Grade II Listed Chambers were converted to offices in 1930, but the building still retains its original imitation Franco-Flemish style, with red and buff bricks, and ornate sculptures (see **blue plaque** here).

Cross over Richmond Hill and on the right corner with St Stephen's Road is the driveway to **Walton House**,

retirement home of William Henry (WH) Smith, now offices. Smith lived here from 1862 until his death in 1865, enjoying a brief retirement in this large villa set in an acre overlooking the sea.

Take St Stephen's Road, passing the rear of Richmond Hill St Andrew's Church. The long red-brick building opposite is called **Fern Bank** and was hit by a bomb on 10 April 1941, killing eight, including poet Cumberland Clark. Ironically he had written 'Let the bombs bounce round above us. And the shells come whizzing by. Down in our air raid shelter. We'll be cosy you and I.'

A little further on your right is **St Stephen's**, one of Dorset's finest Gothic Revival churches. Just before crossing the road bridge, take the steps down to Braidley Road. Opposite is the modern (1990) **Town Hall** Extension, housing the Customer Service Centre. A previous, but somewhat lower incarnation was the Grand Hall function rooms, which in the 1970s hosted events such as the popular ITV wrestling matches with the likes of Mick McManus, Big Daddy and Giant Haystacks. The foundation stone of the original Town Hall, which was the Mont Dore Hotel to begin with, is by the main entrance, laid in 1881 by Oscar II, King of Sweden and Norway.

Continue left to Bourne Avenue which was once called Sanatorium Road, as hidden behind the Italianate Town Hall and mature vegetation is the extensive former Royal National Sanatorium, now **Brompton Court** assisted living apartments.

Cross over into the Central Gardens to see the WWI **cenotaph** (unveiled in 1922), designed by borough deputy architect E.A. Shervey and sculpted from Portland stone by W.A. Hoare. In WWII it survived a German bomb landing just 30 yards away. The two lions are copies of those guarding the tomb of Pope Clement XIII in St Peter's Basilica, Rome. Note, only one of the lions appears to be paying attention, the other being asleep.

We're in the vicinity here of the Decoy Pond, shown on the *Award Map* of 1805, which was about 300 yards from The Square and was a wider part of the Bourne, measuring some 135 × 66 ft. Bourne House was built in 1726, either where today's cenotaph is or further back near The Square; wildfowlers waited here to shoot ducks landing on the pond. In 1838 the house was converted to a chapel and schoolroom.

Walk behind the cenotaph, crossing the stream, and bear left. It is here along Avenue Road (the road above the Gardens) that Britain's worst tram disaster occurred in 1908, a brake failure and derailment causing the tram to fall 20 ft, killing 7 passengers and injuring 26.

Continue left, noting the **WWII plaques**. **Hampshire Court** on Bourne Avenue across the gardens had a popular ground-floor Swiss restaurant in the 1950s. That Swiss connection persists as the town was twinned with Lucerne, Switzerland in 1982.

Just before The Square, turn left, back over the Bourne and walk through the **pergola**, noting its green plaque. Then turn back to The Square and retrace your earlier path to the start of Post Office Road. Continue up Old Christchurch Road.

On reaching The Arcade, note the **blue plaque** to the left of the canopy. This was the site of Bournemouth's **first town hall** (1875), which later became the Criterion Hotel and then the Criterion Arcade (1886). The first-floor stone arch supported the arcade entrance. Under the canopy, the stone below the clock and the clock itself were presented on 1 December 1990 to mark Bournemouth borough's centenary and commemorates the town's links with Lucerne.

Walk through **The Arcade** (previously known as Gervis Arcade, Royal Arcade and Henry Joy's Arcade). Inside, above the entrance, is a **blue plaque** noting this was originally two rows of shops, the glass roof being added in 1872. Dubbed 'Joy's Folly' after its creator Henry Joy, the Arcade took 7 years to build (1866–73) and was less than popular as it replaced a pretty glen and rustic bridge.

Exit at Gervis Place and cross the road. Look back at the elaborate arcade entrance. The circular structures either side once had cupolas above.

Cross over **Westover Road**, which was the main residential road in Bournemouth in its early days, and the first to be improved and gravelled in 1857. The road gained a reputation as

the 'Bond Street of Bournemouth' and best street outside London, although the closure of the ABC and Odeon cinemas and the Ice Rink reduced footfall significantly. The Grade II Listed **Westover Gardens Hotel** (*c* 1900) can be seen here, but is now student accommodation.

The newish building occupied by **The Stable** bar and restaurant used

to house the TIC, which opened in 1990 and then moved to Bournemouth Pier. The 1990 TIC had a pair of blue plaques commemorating both the opening of the new building and the original Information Bureau (provided and operated by Bournemouth Chamber of Trade, 1928–48). Before that the building was allegedly a stables, hence the aptly named establishment today.

To the right, go down the slope and enter the Lower Gardens. This is **Pine Walk** (formerly Invalids' Walk), which runs roughly parallel to Westover Road and behind the current 1933 **bandstand** (replacing one of 1884), which has a marriage licence. The part of **the Bourne** below the bandstand was known as Children's Corner, where youngsters, including Winston Churchill, used to sail model boats. The boggy fields either side of the Bourne were drained in the 1840s to create today's Gardens, with promenades and paths added during the 1860s and 1870s. A design competition in 1870 for the Lower Gardens was won by Mr Tree! A fountain with a 40-ft-diameter basin was installed and electric lighting was added in 1899 to illuminate the Gardens.

Before reaching the Pavilion and rock garden, take the left path up to the **aviary** and enjoy a stroll past the birds and **art exhibition** (if it's the season for this). Bear left to exit the Gardens and head right up Westover Road, passing the former ABC Cinema and Westover Ice Rink.

Facing the **Pavilion** is the former **Gaumont/Odeon cinema** with its ornate arcading. Built and designed primarily as a cinema, it opened on 13 May 1929 as the Regent Theatre, just 2 months after the Pavilion. Its auditorium seated almost 2,300. It closed in Feb 2017 when the new BH2 Leisure Centre opened

The old seafront in the early 1930s. (Courtesy of Bournemouth Libraries.) The sign above the central door read 'These buildings erected in 1876 will be demolished at the end of the 1934 season …'.

on Exeter Road. The Casino next door used to be Motor Mac's Garage, an impressive car dealership in keeping with the then-affluent area. Next is a **Premier Inn**, formerly the Palace Court Hotel (1936), with its Art Deco balconies and ocean-going liner appearance.

At the roundabout, bear right and cross over **Bath Road**. Hotels and boarding houses once stood where today's Bath Road South car park is. One of these was Kildare, where Fabian writer Beatrice Webb spent three winters. She was here when she received her first article acceptance. Further down the hill on the left, there had been a Bath House and shops. This was replaced by the New Baths (1937–84) (later known as Pier Approach Baths), whose frontage was roughly level with the start of the flyover.

The Waterfront Complex 1998–2013. (© Chris Downer, Geograph cc-by-sa/2.0.)

A later structure here was the Waterfront complex and IMAX, which gained architectural notoriety for the wrong reasons, and was quickly demolished. After many years vacant, the site was chosen for a rather impressive Smugglers' Cove Adventure Mini-Golf.

Head for the **seafront** by a path at the end of the car park, then take the steps down by Harry Ramsden's. Bear left along the promenade. The stone **Undercliff Cloisters** were built in 'Roman-style' in 1907 when the first part of Undercliff Drive was opened. A little further on, look out for the blue plaque on the **beach hut**, as the first municipal hut was built in Bournemouth in 1909.

Double-back towards the pier, noting the **stone memorial** at the end of the rockery just beyond the Cloisters, which commemorates the opening of Undercliff Drive. Today's Edwardian **pier** benefited from electric lighting in

1899 and a landing-stage extension in 1909, and 'celebrated' its centenary in 1980 by having badly corroded ironwork on the foreshore replaced with reinforced concrete. The remodelled two-storey octagonal entrance opened in 1981. Take a walk to the end of the pier, where you'll find a café with spectacular views along the coast. There is a pier toll during peak season (end March to end October).

Back at Pier Approach, part of the **Oceanarium** used to be a Victorian Gentleman's Club ('Bournemouth Club'), one of the oldest remaining beach buildings.

On the wall of the **flyover** (built in 1972) is a plaque about the town's sewerage! Tucked under the flyover is the AIDS Wall (and plaque).

Return to Pier Approach and head up past **Hot Rocks**, which is on the site of the Bourne Bay Hotel. There's a neat photo opportunity using the mural outside the bar restaurant.

Next is **Court Royal**, once the Madeira Hotel, where, in 1898, Guglielmo Marconi stayed, setting up his laboratory in a cellar and erecting a 100- to

125-ft aerial mast to receive the first paid 'radiogram' from Lord Kelvin on the Isle of Wight. Possibly due to all the disruption he'd caused, Mr Marconi had to quit the Madeira for another guesthouse (Sandhills) further up the cliff! In 1947 Court Royal became a convalescent home for South Wales miners.

Outside the BIC, note the **double-sided statue** of Lewis Tregonwell and Christopher Crabb Creeke. On the other side of the road is **Park Central Hotel**, originally Vale Royal Hotel (1890s), before becoming Punshon Methodist Church House in the late 1940s, with a modernist Methodist church opening next door in 1958, which was later demolished. Church House was later used as an Adult Education Centre before becoming a hotel once more in 2009. Finish the walk back at the Royal Exeter Hotel.

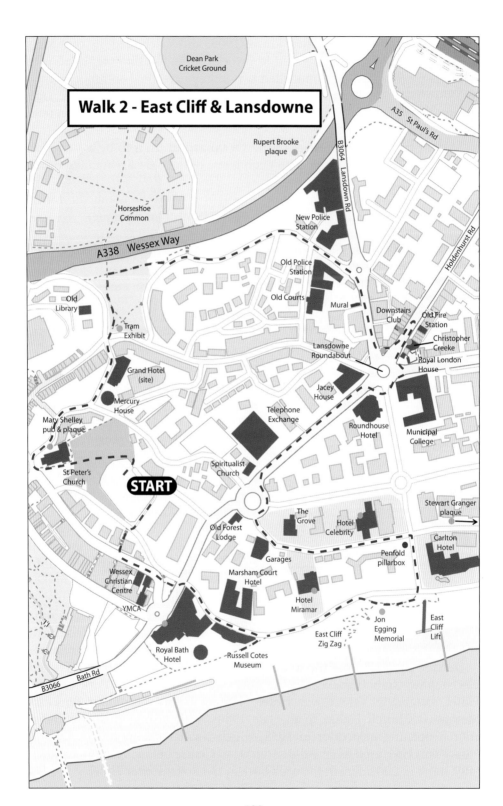

Walk 2 - East Cliff & Lansdowne

Dean Park
Cricket Ground

Rupert Brooke
plaque

Horseshoe
Common

New Police
Station

A338   Wessex Way

Old Police
Station

Old
Library

Old Courts

Mural

Downstairs
Club

Old Fire
Station

Tram
Exhibit

Lansdowne
Roundabout

Christopher
Creeke

Royal London
House

Grand Hotel
(site)

Jacey
House

Mercury
House

Telephone
Exchange

Roundhouse
Hotel

Municipal
College

Mary Shelley
pub & plaque

St Peter's
Church

START

Spiritualist
Church

Stewart Granger
plaque

The
Grove

Hotel
Celebrity

Old Forest
Lodge

Carlton
Hotel

Garages

Penfold
pillarbox

Wessex
Christian
Centre

Marsham Court
Hotel

YMCA

Hotel
Miramar

Jon
Egging
Memorial

East
Cliff
Lift

East Cliff
Zig Zag

Royal Bath
Hotel

Russell Cotes
Museum

B3066   Bath Rd

B3064

Lansdown Rd

A35   St Paul's Rd

Holdenhurst Rd

Walk 2: East Cliff and Lansdowne

Start and finish: Central car park,
Upper Hinton Road, BH1 2HH
Approx. distance: 3.5 km

Exit the car park down the access road, then cross over Upper Hinton Road and take the steps down to Hinton Road. Measured at just 10 m in length, this could be the borough's shortest public thoroughfare. The 'Exit' door ahead of you was from the old Gaumont cinema on Westover Road.

Turn left. The car park entrance used to be the back of Motor Mac's Garage car dealership on Westover Road. **Wessex Christian Centre** (the 'Discover' Church) was once the Playhouse Theatre. Next door notice the elaborate doorway to the **Cairns Memorial YMCA Building** (the entrance to the current YMCA is on Westover Road). Aptly, the Cairns motto 'Effloresco' means to bloom or flourish.

At the end of the road pause to admire the slightly faded grandeur of the Classical-style **Royal Bath Hotel**, which has been extended several times since it was built in 1838. Bear left up hill, crossing Bath Road and taking the first right (Russell Cotes Road).

Marsham Court Hotel was built in 1913, the first owners reputedly a Mr and Mrs Marsh who owned a ham-curing business (hence the name Marsh-ham). By 1923, demand for rooms had increased, so the neighbouring house was purchased and linked, increasing capacity to 41 rooms. In 1937 the hotel was owned by Quakers, so it was a temperance hotel, like the Granville on Richmond Hill. During WWII it was taken over by the US Red Cross, as a convalescent home for wounded soldiers. The hotel was refurbished in the late 1980s, becoming part of the Days Hotel Group, and renamed Marsham Court Hotel in 2015.

When you reach the far end of the **Russell-Cotes Museum**, bear right, down the cliff path, to the museum entrance. The house was built for the Russell-Cotes to hold their collection and also to entertain on a large scale. In 1907 they presented the house and contents to the Corporation of Bournemouth, continuing to reside there until they both died in 1922. Look out for the seaside 'items' on the fence and admire the view of the pier from here.

Return to Russell Cotes Road and bear right to follow East Overcliff Drive. J.R.R. Tolkien was a regular guest of the **Hotel Miramar**. A little further on is the top of the **Zig-Zag**, where you often see lizards in the undergrowth. The memorial to Red Arrow pilot **Jon Egging**, who died at Bournemouth Air Show in August 2011, was moved here after a major slip on the East Cliff in April 2016, which also put the lift out of operation.

Continue on to the **East Cliff Lift** and its upper viewing platform, set into the clifftop, 110 ft above sea level. The platform once had an overhanging 'promenade'. The lift opened in April 1908, but the old cars were replaced in 2007, increasing their capacity from 10 to 12. A landslip in April 2016 requires extensive and expensive cliff stabilization before the lift can reopen.

Turn left into Meyrick Road. The **Carlton Hotel** here has been welcoming holidaymakers since 1903. There is a rare example of a **Penfold pillar box**, named after designer John Penfold, at the corner of Meyrick Road and Grove Road, which has stood here since 1876.

Take Grove Road, and on your right is the **Hotel Celebrity**, previously Durlston Court Hotel, which Tony Hancock's family used to run (there is a blue plaque by the front entrance). The corridors and 59 rooms have celebrity themes.

Towards the end of Grove Road, the green-roofed building is **The Grove** (see interview in History chapter about this unique hotel). Glance left at the roundabout to see Marsham Court Hotel's interesting old **garages**. Ahead is another of Bournemouth's old properties, **Old Forest Lodge**, home for 35 years to Rosemary Tonks, post-war 'literary star of London' and 'the poet who vanished'.

Across the roundabout is **Bournemouth Spiritualist Church**, with its unusual spire, previously a doctor's house and surgery before opening as a church in 1924. Next is the former **Telephone Exchange** (*c* 1954), now offices. There's a depiction of Hermes/Mercury on the right-hand end, the Greek/Roman god of communication.

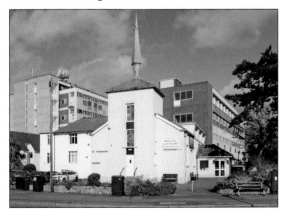

At the Lansdowne roundabout, pause to admire some of the historic buildings here. **Jacey House** was once the Queen Hotel (1891) and is now apartments. The **Roundhouse** was the first new hotel in Bournemouth since 1938, built in 1969 on the site of the old Imperial, a grand Victorian hotel. Across Meyrick Road is Bournemouth & Poole's **Municipal College** with its landmark chiming clock tower.

Across again on Christchurch Road, **Royal London House** was built on the site of the old Metropole Hotel, which was hit by a bomb on 23 May 1943 which killed many airmen billeted there. It reopened 4 months later but was finally demolished in 1955. Royal London House used to have a Fortes coffee shop on the ground floor (now KFC).

Proceed round the roundabout to Holdenhurst Road. On the right is the **Christopher Creeke pub** and **plaque**, named after one of Bournemouth's early surveyors.

Walk a little further and you will

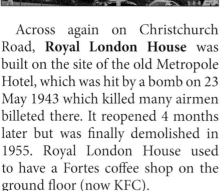

see the **Old Fire Station**, one of the town's first fire stations, but now a night club. Cross the road, and head back towards the roundabout. Opposite the Christopher Creeke is a blue plaque to the **Downstairs Club** (basement of No. 9), Bournemouth's first full-time rock venue in 1961, where popstars such as Manfred Mann, Eric Clapton, The Who and Georgie Fame once performed.

Bear right into the small Lansdowne Crescent in front of the post office where there is a **memorial** to those who died in the 1943 air raid. Bear right again, into Lansdowne Road. Don't miss the colourful **mural** on the left.

At the roundabout note the rapidly expanding number, and height, of the buildings in this area. Many are **student accommodation**, and bottle collections in the windows suggest student life doesn't change.

Turn left into Madeira Road and the old Police Station is on your left and the imposing new **Police Station** on your right. Glance down Stafford Road to see the **old court** buildings, which have been relocated behind the hospital in Littledown.

Towards the end of Madeira Road take the unmarked steps (right) down into **Horseshoe Common**. If you pop under the Wessex Way flyover, there is a small pond to enjoy. Directly across the Common on Dean Park Crescent is the **Old Library House**, an early-Victorian villa which was the Central Library in 1901.

The southern end of Horseshoe Common at Old Christchurch Road is an up-and-coming part of Bournemouth, with 20 mph limits and night-time partial road closures to allow people to enjoy the area. The prominent Citrus Building is another example of the increasing investment/development by the Bournemouth Development Company.

As well as its shape, the Common may have got its name from the horseshoe-shaped cast-iron underground yokes of the conduit system used by trams of

the Bournemouth Electric Tramway; there is an informative **plaque** next to the Electric Idea sculpture.

Cross over Old Christchurch Road into Fir Vale Road. One of Bournemouth's largest hotels, the aptly named **Grand Hotel**, used to be here where South Western House is today. It was demolished in 1962.

Grand Hotel c 1923. (Courtesy of Bournemouth Libraries.)

Mercury House, the round building, was built in 1973 on the site of Compton House Hotel. D.H. Lawrence stayed here in January 1912 on his doctor's advice (a year before *Sons and Lovers* was published). Mercury House now offers accommodation to students.

Bear right into St Peter's Road past Burlington Arcade. Round the corner is a long, low building, the **Mary Shelley (Wetherspoon's)**. It was formerly a J.J. Allen store, selling house furnishings.

Opposite, a blue **plaque** on the wall below **St Peter's** is dedicated to Mary Shelley and family. Enter the churchyard. The church is built of Purbeck stone and has an elegant 202-ft spire (half the height of Salisbury Cathedral spire) and is well worth a visit. Inside, it is very colourful, with painted walls and ceilings and also lovely wood-covered ceilings. There is a cafe with comfy settees, a perfect end to your walk perhaps. Outside, note the 22-ft-high cross, and separate Chapel of the Resurrection designed by Sir Ninian Comper.

Walk through the churchyard, looking out for the famous **graves** shown on the information board. These include the Shelley and Tregonwell tombs, plus the grave of Major-General Richard Moody, founder of British Columbia. The **Shelley tomb** contains six family members, if we include Percy Bysshe Shelley's heart, while the Tregonwell tomb also commemorates six family members.

At the back of the churchyard, ascend the steps erected by the church's founder, Rev Morden Bennett. There are 39 steps –

nothing to do with John Buchan's famous book *The Thirty-Nine Steps*, but everything to do with the 39 Articles (which form the basic summary of the belief of the Church of England). The steps lead you back to the Central car park.

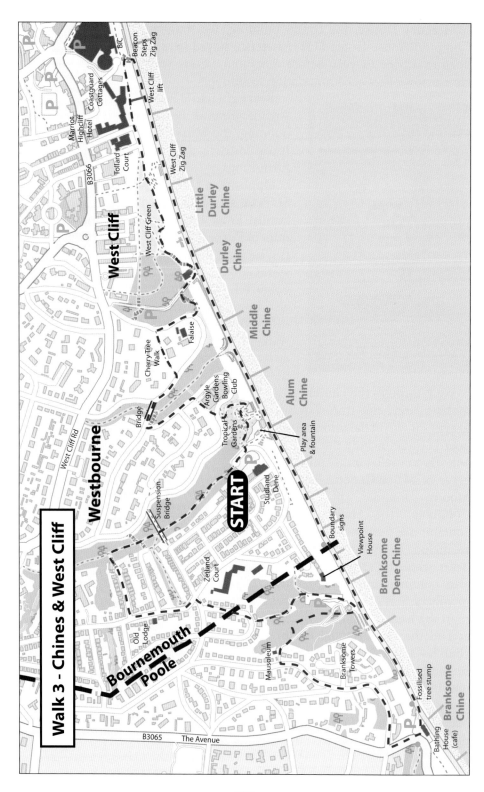

Walk 3 - Chines & West Cliff

West Cliff

Westbourne

Bournemouth
Poole

BIC
Beacon Steps Zig Zag
West Cliff lift
Coastguard Cottages
Marriot Highcliff Hotel
Tollard Court
B3066
West Cliff Zig Zag
Little Durley Chine
West Cliff Green
Durley Chine
Falaise
Middle Chine
Cherry Tree Walk
Argyle Gardens
Bowling Club
Alum Chine
Bridge
Tropical Gardens
Play area & fountain
West Cliff Rd
Suspension Bridge
START
Studland Dene
Boundary signs
Viewpoint House
Zetland Court
Branksome Dene Chine
Old Lodge
Mausoleum
Branksome Towers
Fossilised tree stump
B3065   The Avenue
Bathing House (cafe)
Branksome Chine

136

Walk 3: Chines and West Cliff

Start and finish: Alum Chine car park, BH4 8DP
Approx. distance: 7.5 km

Alum Chine is a favourite beach for locals, away from the hustle and bustle of the Pier and town centre, particularly loved for its wide, clean, sandy beach. Make your way up the chine to the suspension bridge known as **Stevenson Memorial Bridge**, built in 1904. This features in Cyril Connolly's book *The Unquiet Grave* (1944).

Continue up the chine, following the lower right-hand path until you come to some steep steps on the left with an ornate metal gantry. Climb these up into Rosemount Road, and walk up to Alumhurst Road. Turn left and 50 m on your right is the Grade II Listed **Old Lodge**, with its original decorative barge-boards and ridges, which marked the entrance to the original driveway of Branksome Dene, a large house a little further

down the road (now **Zetland Court**). The house overlooks Branksome Dene Chine and was part of a 50-acre estate. It was built in 1860 for Charles A. King, churchwarden of St Peter's. The building was vastly enlarged for Lord Wimborne (a steel magnate) as his seaside home. The Prince of Wales (Edward VII) enjoyed lunch here in 1890 when opening the Royal Victoria Hospital. Young Winston Churchill stayed here too, as Lord Wimborne was his uncle. The house was bought by Sir

Zetland Court. (Courtesy of RMBI Care Co. Home Zetland Court.)

Ernest Cassel, a millionaire financier of German descent, and enlarged again for him *c* 1913–14. The next owner, by inheritance, was his granddaughter Edwina, who married Lord Mountbatten. The building became Britain's first vegetarian hotel *c* 1927, a billet for the Canadian Air Force (1943), then a convalescent home (1951) and a Jewish retirement home. It was renamed Zetland Court and in 1983 became a Royal Masonic Benevolent Institution (RMBI) care home.

Turn right into Mountbatten Road, then immediately left into horseshoe-shaped Cassel Avenue, entering Poole before reaching the bottom of the horseshoe. Just before the road doubles back, take the footpath (No. 64) into **Branksome Dene Chine**. Follow the path through this 13-acre nature reserve

to reach the bottom of the chine, where there is an information board.

Bear right towards the white building (toilets and **Community Room**). Facing the sea, above a flight of steps to the promenade, is a **plaque** recording the opening of the chine in July 1928.

Head back into the car park and take the steps ahead by the no-entry sign for an excellent view of imposing **Viewpoint House**, the white house overlooking the chine. This was built in the 1930s and was the home of entertainer Max Bygraves for 33 years until 2003. It is thought to be one of several secret locations used for D-Day planning. The chine meanwhile was used for commando training during WWII. The author J.R.R. Tolkien and composer Mantovani also lived in this affluent Branksome Park area.

Proceed along the path, past a rope swing, and descend the steps back to the access road. At the top of the chine is the **Packe Family Mausoleum**, which occasionally opens to the public. The Listed mausoleum (restored in the early 1990s) is all that remains of the once large Branksome Tower estate, laid out in the mid-19th century for Charles William Packe, a Leicestershire MP. In 1853 he bought 745 acres extending as far as County Gates (originally

Packe Gates), in Westbourne, where a lodge marked the entrance to the long drive (now called the Avenue) leading to his mansion Branksome Tower, which once stood south of the mausoleum on the clifftop. When Charles King moved into nearby Branksome Dene, Packe and King seem to have fallen out. In a case of 'manorial turf wars', Packe ordered an embankment to be built, planting it with trees to block King's view. Legal proceedings ensued, and Packe was obliged to lower its height.

Packe's mansion was sold in 1892 and became Branksome Tower Hotel. Shortly before WWII, German General Werner von Blomberg stayed here and busied himself photographing Poole Bay (a possible invasion site). In 1973 the hotel was demolished despite public outcry and the site has since been developed into the **Branksome Towers** private estate, with a mix of houses and four matching apartment blocks dominating the cliff.

Exit the chine onto Pinewood Road. Turn left, following Pinewood Road, which becomes Westminster Road. Pass the entrance to Branksome Towers estate. The gates to No 8A Westminster Road are believed to be the original ones from the Estate. This property is also unusual, as it effectively has its own mini-chine down to the beach, which can be seen if footpath No 66 is passable. Across the crossroads at the end of Westminster Road is Lakeside Road where at **No. 19**, J.R.R. Tolkien had his retirement home (Woodridings), now replaced by two houses by the names of Beren and Luthien (characters in the works of Tolkien, later published as a standalone book, 2017).

Turn left towards **Branksome Chine**. The chine itself is across the road beside Lakeside Road and is a long woodland walk between the seafront and the Penn Hill area of Poole. At the entrance to the chine is a **plaque** commemorating its opening in September 1930 by Margaret Bondfield, Minister of Labour and Britain's first female cabinet minister. Poet John Betjeman wrote: 'walk the asphalt paths of Branksome Chine/In resin scented air like strong Greek wine'.

Head across the road into the car park. The **white-and-blue building** offered changing rooms for sea-bathers; it was also the UK's first solarium, offering sunbathers the chance to absorb 'the health-giving beams of the artificial sun' inside, all year round, or, if they preferred the real thing, to sit in the tea-lounge beneath the 'Vita-glass'. The solarium wasn't to British tastes though, and the building was later turned into a popular seaside cafe.

Turn left along the promenade and start walking back towards Bournemouth. Just past the Surf Lifesaving Club note the **fossilised tree stump** by the steps. It was placed here in 2009 and is believed to be from a tree that was living some 140 million years ago. The information board

mentions naturalist Alfred Russel Wallace, who lived in nearby Broadstone and worked on theories of evolution and natural selection contemporaneously with Charles Darwin. Further along the promenade is a **mural**, part of the Bournemouth and Poole Selfie Wall Trail.

After passing Branksome Dene Chine, pause at the modern blue 'Welcome to Bournemouth Seafront' sign and the opposing and far more decorative 'Welcome to Poole', marking the **borough boundary**. A bronze **plaque** here describes how the Society of Poole Men would 'beat the bounds'.

Further on by **beach hut No. 228** is a stone commemorating the extension of Alum Chine Promenade in October 1957. At the **stone arches and Seafront Office** is more Selfie Wall Trail art, this time by Ricky 'Also' Walker.

Now back at Alum Chine, you're on an earlier extension to the promenade (Bournemouth Pier to Alum Chine), opened in 1930 by Ellen Cooper-Dean. Carry on along the promenade, past **Middle Chine** and **Durley Chine**. Just past the Harvester is the **Lifeguard Corps portacabin**; this part of the beach

is lifeguarded between May and September. You'll also pass some toilets at the base of an inlet called **Little Durley Chine**, which is now used as one of the council's waste transfer stations and as a depot for the council's beach vehicles. This was once the site of Joseph's Steps, another way up the cliffs.

Walk beyond **West Cliff Zig-Zag** to **West Cliff Lift**. If it is operating you may either take this or go on to the next zig-zag (**Beacon Steps**), just before the Amusements, and ascend the cliff. You'll emerge at the top, facing the Purbeck Hall of the BIC. Turn left and pass the top of the lift.

The **Marriott Highcliff** (the 'e' was dropped to avoid confusion with Highcliffe, Christchurch) on your right began as Highcliffe Mansions, four elegant properties which were joined together to become the Highcliff Hotel in 1874. An important meeting occurred here in 1940 when the NEC (National Executive Committee), under Labour leader Clement Attlee, agreed to join a National Government, but not under PM Neville Chamberlain. Within hours, Winston Churchill was asked to form a government. Post-war PMs Jim Callaghan, Margaret Thatcher, John Major and Tony Blair have all stayed here for their conferences in Bournemouth. The hotel even played its part in US politics, as it was here that Senator John McCain announced his intention to run for President a year before losing to Barack Obama. At the back of the gardens are the former coastguard cottages. The Government established a coastguard 1831, to combat smuggling.

Beyond the Marriott is the former **Tollard Royal Hotel**, now apartments. One unwelcome resident in July 1946 was Neville Heath, who was executed in October 1946 for murdering two women, one of them Doreen Marshall who was holidaying in Bournemouth. The Tollard Royal's copper-sheathed dome was added in 1928. There is an interesting board here describing the various architectural styles to be seen in West Cliff and Poole Hill Conservation Area.

Continue straight ahead into **West Cliff Green**, taking the left-hand path, past the cafe, which leads to Durley Chine Steps and down the cliff (joggers use them as training steps). On reaching the bottom, walk a short way up the chine and take the steps on the left up to West Overcliff Drive. Across the road is a large house called **Falaise**. This was the home of pioneering aviator Sir Alan Cobham in the 1950s and 1960s. When Cobham was BSO chairman, Sir Charles Groves conducted the orchestra here in the garden.

Head right along the road, then left onto **Cherry Tree Walk** ornamental path, especially lovely in spring. At the end of the Walk, turn right, then left, crossing the bridge over Middle Chine. If you wish to visit the chine, take the steps just beyond the bridge, walk down the chine, but return the same way.

Continue left, following West Overcliff Drive. Turn right into Argyll Gardens and pass **Argyll Bowling Club**, founded 1905 and one of three clubs that have occupied the West Cliff and Alum Chine area since the late 1800s. The Argyll name probably comes from R.L. Stevenson's family and business link to Argyll, Scotland. There is a public café where you can pick up a Plant Trail of the Tropical Gardens.

Cross West Overcliff Drive again and take the zig-zag path down into Alum Chine **Tropical Gardens**. There are numerous information boards listing the plants and history.

Studland Dene apartments overlooking the chine on the far side are built on the site of a former hotel, which was used as a rest centre for bombed-out mothers and babies during WWII, especially from heavily targeted cities like Bristol.

At the seafront you'll find a playground, Vesuvio bar and restaurant, toilets and turning area for the land train. Apparently, there was once a jetty here where boats could be hired. Next to the play area entrance is a blue Handyside **drinking fountain** which dates to the 1880s. Walk inland, up the chine, to complete the Walk.

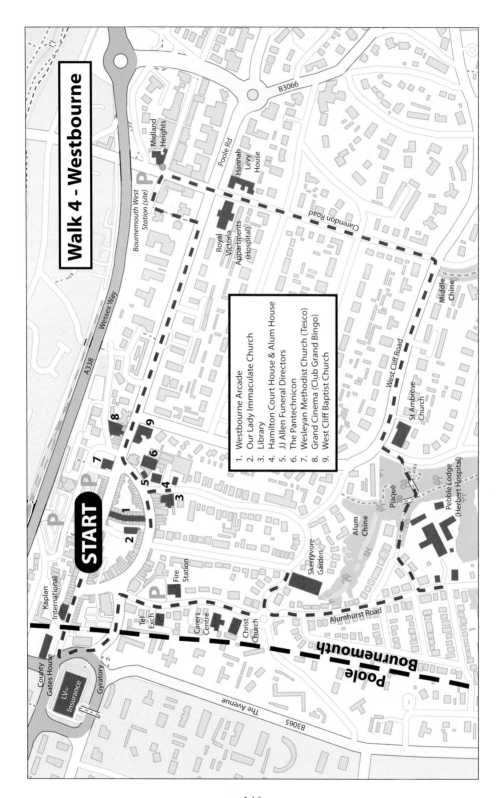

Walk 4 - Westbourne

START

1. Westbourne Arcade
2. Our Lady Immaculate Church
3. Library
4. Hamilton Court House & Alum House
5. JJ Allen Funeral Directors
6. The Pantechnicon
7. Wesleyan Methodist Church (Tesco)
8. Grand Cinema (Club Grand Bingo)
9. West Cliff Baptist Church

Bournemouth West Station (site)

Midland Heights

Poole Rd

Hannah Levy House

Royal Victoria Appartments (Hospital)

Clarendon Road

B3066

Wessex Way

A338

Kaplan International

County Gates House

LV= Insurance

Gyratory

Tel Exch

Fire Station

Carers Centre

Christ Church

Skerryvore Garden

Alumhurst Road

The Avenue

B3065

Poole
Bournemouth

Alum Chine

Plaque

Pebble Lodge (Herbert Hospital)

St Ambrose Church

West Cliff Road

Middle Chine

146

Walk 4: Westbourne

Start and finish: Entrance to Westbourne Arcade (Poole Road end)
Approx. distance: 4 km

Grade II Listed **Westbourne Arcade** was built in 1884/85 in Gothic style by Henry Joy, who also built Gervis Arcade in Bournemouth. It has symmetrical entrances in Poole Road and Seamoor Road, with three round-headed arches, the centre one shorter and half-glazed. Joy lived in Seamoor House on Poole Road (now demolished). Halfway through the Arcade, on the left, is the **Vintage Lounge** (coffee/art house), which has the Colosseum in its basement, the UK's smallest cinema.

At the end of the Arcade go right on Seamoor Road to see an archway leading to **Our Lady Immaculate Church**. This was once the entrance to a market (the church later occupying the site).

Retrace your steps to the Arcade, then cross over Seamoor Road. Head left past the Post Office, then turn right into Alum Chine Road. On the right is the Grade II Listed **library** (1912), which has an

attractive half-timbered gable at the front with plasterwork coat of arms.

Cross over Alum Chine Road and note the rather fine **Hamilton Court House** and **Alum House**. Return to Seamoor Road and bear right. On your right is Westbourne Funeralcare part of the Cooperative Funeral business,

but this particular branch still includes the much older **J.J. Allen Funeral Directors**. This single-storey Italianate cream-washed brick stucco pavilion dates to around 1860 and is Grade II Listed.

The imposing building behind is the **Pantechnicon**, built a decade later in Italian medieval style and also Grade II Listed. This three-storey warehouse

was used by J.J. Allen as part of its removals business. In 2003 the building was converted into luxury flats and business units.

At the end of Seamoor Road, directly across Poole Road, you will see **Wesleyan Methodist Church** (1898–2009), now a local supermarket and eatery.

Head right along Poole Road. The church on the right is the Grade II Listed (1891) **West Cliff Baptist Church**, or Baptist tabernacle, which has three bay aisles and a gallery over its entrance at the north end. There was provision for galleries over the aisles, which were not built. It is attached to a large hall or schoolroom to the west.

Directly opposite is yet another Grade II Listed building, the former **Grand Cinema** (1922–75). One of the 'super cinemas' from the 1920s, it was designed by H.E. Hawker. The Grand became a star itself, used as an interior location for the film *Valentino* (1977) when it doubled-up as a New York picture house. From 1978 to January 2018 the building was used as a bingo club.

Continue east along Poole Road and about 50 m before the traffic lights look out for a path on the left, just after a wooden fence, between Bourne Hall and Holly Court/Ivy House. Take the path down the hill to the coach

Bournemouth West Station 1963. (Source: Ben Brooksbank, Wikimedia Commons.)

and car park. You are on the site of the former **Bournemouth West terminus station** (1874). The Somerset and Dorset railway line finished here and the entrance would have been to the right off Queen's Road, and the platforms where the coach park is today, with tracks coming in from the west. The station closed in 1965, but some of the retaining walls can still be discerned. The Bournemouth Train Care Depot was built just to the west of here, on the approaches to Bournemouth West.

Directly across Queen's Road is **Midland Heights** apartments, formerly Midland Hotel *c* 1800. The **plaque** near the door states this was Bournemouth's first railway hotel.

Follow Queen's Road, up the hill, back to Poole Road. Across the road, on the right corner with Clarendon Road is **Royal Victoria Apartments** (behind trees). It was felt a new hospital was needed to meet the needs of people in west Bournemouth and its foundation stone was laid on 21 June 1887, the Golden Jubilee of Queen Victoria, who gave her permission for it to be called the Royal Victoria. The hospital was officially opened by her son Edward, the Prince of Wales, on 16 January 1890 (there is a stone commemorating this to the left of the main entrance). A children's ward was opened by the Duchess of Argyll in January 1903. The building on the other corner of Clarendon Road is **Hannah Levy House**, a Jewish care home since 1956.

Take Clarendon Road, all the way to West Cliff Road. Turn right here passing the entrance to **Middle Chine**. Many of the earlier Victorian villas have been replaced with apartment blocks in this area.

St Ambrose, the parish church of Westbourne, was built in 1898–1900 by C. Hodgson Fowler of Durham on land given by the Cooper-Dean family. This wasn't the first St Ambrose church; its predecessor, opened 18 years previously in Alumhurst Road, was described as 'big but undistinguished'. Perhaps a church of more handsome design was wanted, to be more uplifting. The old St Ambrose is now a carers centre.

Turn left into West Overcliff Drive, cross the road and at the shelter take the footpath and steps down into **Alum Chine**. Cross the chine by the pedestrian bridge and bear right to see the **plaque** to Robert Louis Stevenson, whose home Skerryvore overlooked the top of the chine.

Ignore the second bridge and take the path uphill to the left. Exit Alum Chine, go left along Drury Road, then left onto Alumhurst Road.

The Grade II listed **Herbert Hospital**, also known as Pebble Lodge, was originally the Herbert Memorial Convalescent Home, and was built between 1865 and 1867 by T.H. Wyatt in Gothic style, on a 4-acre plot of the Alum Chine Estate. It was named as a memorial to Lord Sidney Herbert of Lea

Herbert Lodge and Herbert House. (Courtesy of Dorset Healthcare Trust.) Site access is strictly via Reception.

(Secretary of State for War 1852–55), who was a close friend of Florence Nightingale, whom he had asked to go and nurse in the Crimea, and who would play an active part in the Hospital's design. At the time, the hospital was only the third building on the lonely heathland comprising today's Westbourne, the others being Branksome Dene (now Zetland Court (1860)) and Branksome Tower (1855). During WWII, servicemen came to the hospital for convalescence. The building has a porch tower with statue, clock and short spire, and Italianate stucco chimneys. An Edwardian white timber summerhouse (c 1910) is detached from the main building, as is the stone entrance Lodge. Today the building is occupied by various NHS departments and privacy should be respected.

Turn around and head back up Alumhurst Road. At the roundabout bear right to see **Skerryvore**, the site of Robert Louis Stevenson's home and now a public garden. The house was destroyed in an air raid in November 1940. There

is a small stone lighthouse in commemoration, as it was named after Skerryvore Lighthouse (the tallest in Scotland), near Tiree, Argyll, surveyed by his great uncle Robert and then built by his uncle Alan Stevenson. Adelaide Anne Boodle visited the Stevensons here and wrote a novel of Robert's life, while resident in Westbourne (*R.L.S. and his Sine Qua Non: Flashlights from Skerryvore by the Gamekeeper*, published 1926).

Turn back to the roundabout and bear right onto Alumhurst Road. Along this road you pass **Christ Church** (built in 1913 and a fine example of Arts and Crafts ecclesiastical architecture), **Bournemouth and Poole Carers Centre** (formerly St Ambrose Church), the **fire station** and old **telephone exchange**.

At the traffic lights go left (on Seamoor Road), then bear right around the busy County Gates Gyratory with the Liverpool Victoria (LV) HQ at its centre. This and the **County Gates House** office block ahead are reminders of the historic pre-1974 boundary between Dorset and Hampshire. When local government was reorganised and Bournemouth (and Christchurch) moved into Dorset on 1 April 1974 the boundary became that between the boroughs of Poole and Bournemouth. This area also marks the entrance to the former Branksome Tower Estate, with today's 'The Avenue' being its lengthy driveway.

Bear right into Poole Road, where tram lines once ran. The building on the left (**Kaplan International English**) is one of Bournemouth's many English Language colleges. A little further on, there were once lavatories in the middle of the road at the junction with Seamoor Road. Finish back at The Arcade.

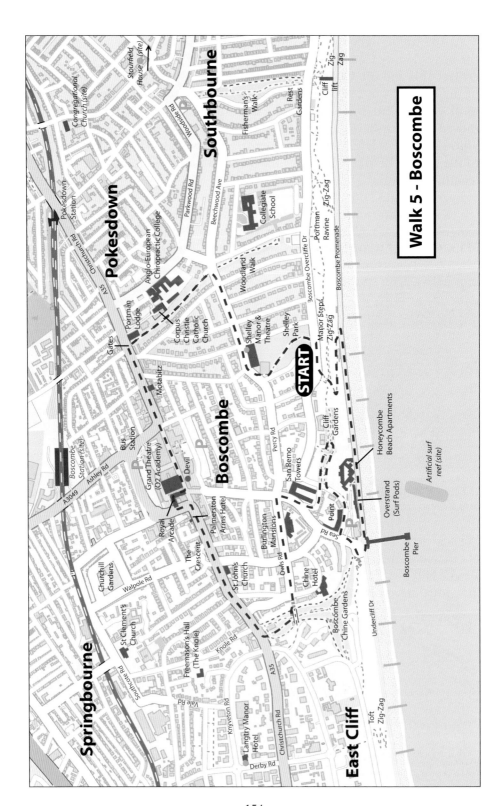

Walk 5 - Boscombe

Southbourne

Pokesdown

Springbourne

Boscombe

East Cliff

Congregational Church (site)

Stourfield House (site)

Fisherman's Walk

Rest Gardens

Cliff Zig-Zag

Lift

Woodside Rd

Parkwood Rd

Beechwood Ave

Collegiate School

Woodland Walk

Anglo-European Chiropractic College

Portman Lodge

Corpus Christie Catholic Church

Shelley Manor & Theatre

Shelley Park

Portman Ravine Zig-Zag

Zig-Zag

Boscombe Overcliffe Dr

Boscombe Promenade

Manor Steps Zig-Zag

Gates

Christchurch Rd

A35

Pokesdown Station

Motabitz

START

Percy Rd

San Remo Towers

Cliff Gardens

Honeycombe Beach Apartments

Artificial surf reef (site)

Boscombe Station (site)

Ashley Rd

A3049

Bus Station

Grand Theatre (O2 Academy)

Devil

Royal Arcade

The Crescent

Palmerston Arms Hotel

Burlington Mansions

Point

Sea Rd

Owls Rd

Overstrand (Surf Pods)

Boscombe Pier

Churchill Gardens

Walpole Rd

St Clement's Church

Southcote Rd

Freemason's Hall (The Knole)

Knole Rd

St John's Church

Chine Hotel

Boscombe Chine Gardens

Undercliff Dr

Vale Rd

Knyveton Rd

Christchurch Rd

A35

Langtry Manor Hotel

Derby Rd

Toft Zig-Zag

154

Walk 5: Boscombe

Start and finish: southern end of Shelley Park, Boscombe Overcliff Drive, BH5 1LN (free parking along this road)
Approx. distance: 3.5 miles (5.5 km)

Take the path towards the cliff, signed to the Beach Lodges. Descend via **Manor Steps Zig-Zag** and turn right along the promenade. Look out for goats grazing on the cliff scrub, introduced in 2009 to help control the invasive non-native plant species.

Just offshore from the **Honeycombe Beach** apartments is the site of the ill-fated artificial surf reef. Note the **Overstrand** building redevelopment, with the retro-modern **pier** very much its centrepiece (Boscombe won the National Piers Society's 'Pier of the Year' in 2010). The late 1950s double-decker block of beach huts has received a modern makeover courtesy of fashion designers Wayne and Gerardine Hemingway. These are now exclusive surf 'pods', with individual retro décor.

Across the road from the pier is **Boscombe Chine Gardens**, with an information board about how they were restored in 2007.

Walk up Sea Road. Undercliff Road to the left still has its **Edwardian houses**, built in 1903. The old Pier Hotel once stood on the right, where artist Aubrey Beardsley stayed in the winter of 1896. The hotel was demolished in 1989 and replaced with **The Point** apartment block. The Allan Bank School for Girls was next door, which later also became a hotel.

Take the first right (The Marina), above Honeycombe Chine (once called Shelley Chine). The chine was filled in and turned into a car park in 1958 and later developed with Honeycombe apartments, named after the chine's honeycomb appearance, caused by wind and rain acting on the sand and clay.

Enjoy a short loop of **Boscombe Cliff Gardens**, with views over the pier; then return to The Marina, heading across into Michelgrove Road. The Italianate **San Remo Towers** (1935–38) were designed by American architect Hector Hamilton, and are the best British example of 'Hacienda' seaside architecture, developed in 1930s Florida. An anti-aircraft battery was positioned on the roof during WWII.

When you reach Sea Road, turn right, then first left into Owls Road, where Burlington Hotel used to be on the left (now **Burlington Mansions**). One of Boscombe's early advocates was Drummond Wolff, who believed it could rival Bournemouth as a watering-hole. He built a villa, Boscombe Towers (1868), where, in 1883, the 'Primrose League', an organisation for spreading Conservative principles in Britain, was founded (the name in memory of Disraeli who loved primroses). This became part of Burlington Hotel, which opened in 1893. The hotel's architect was Thomas Colcutt, who

also designed London's Savoy Hotel. In July 1910 the hotel was used by aviators participating in the Bournemouth Air Pageant. During WWII it became an officer training centre, with the 'Black Watch' also housed here. **Owls Road** was named after a satirical magazine, *The Owl*, founded in 1864 by Sir Algernon Borthwick, a friend and neighbour of Drummond Wolff.

Continue on, but glance down Boscombe Spa Road to your left. The black-and-white **Chine Hotel** was formerly Boscombe Spa Hotel, erected in 1874 by Drummond Wolff to cater for the expected increase in visitors. Famous guests have included Laurel and Hardy, Norman Wisdom, Harry Secombe and Peter Sellers.

Take the path into **Boscombe Chine Gardens** straight ahead of you, with steps down. Below the bridge is a small **pond and water play area**, all that remains of a once-large boating pond. From the footbridge, take the steps down and walk north to the top of the chine. This part of the gardens looked quite different in the 1950s, when there were several tennis courts here.

Turn right and walk up Christchurch Road. After the brow of the hill, the imposing **St John's Church** comes into view, built in 1894 in faux 14th-century style. Almost opposite is **The Crescent** (1868); originally Carnarvon Crescent (after the 4th Earl of Carnarvon, a friend of Drummond Wolff), it was once known as the 'gateway to Boscombe' and there was a bandstand here until the 1950s.

Palmerston Arms Hotel (now **Palmerston Arms Court**) on the left is on the site of one of Boscombe's earliest buildings, the old Ragged Cat pub (1850s). The first floor and double pediment of the old hotel have survived. Opposite was Bournemouth Public Dispensary (1859), which gave free

medical and surgical advice to the town's poor, and the Provident Dispensary Boscombe (1876), located over a shop at 4 Gervis Terrace. The following year, Boscombe, Pokesdown and Springbourne Infirmary opened in Shelley Road, with Sir Percy and Lady Shelley prominent supporters.

Follow the road round to the left into Palmerston Road. The corner where McDonalds is today was once occupied by the splendid Salisbury Hotel (1890), which was demolished in the late 1960s.

Enter the **Royal Arcade** (1892) on your right. We're lucky to still have this, as fire swept through it in 1911, causing £1,800 worth of damage. Organ recitals were once held using the balcony and shoppers continued to listen to music until around 1930, while surrounded by palms and cacti. Note also the octagonal dome in the ceiling. Walk through the 336-ft L-shaped arcade, which turns sharply right to arrive at the pedestrianised section of Christchurch Road.

Exit the arcade and look back at both the arcade (originally the Grand Continental Arcade) and the old **Grand Theatre** (1895), which has its entrance to the right (today's O2 Academy). The trio of hotel, arcade and theatre was the work of Archibald Beckett. Not everyone was happy at having a theatre (bawdy and improper), so the **devil** you see atop the building opposite is a pointed protest (1896) by those who wanted a church built instead.

Continue along Christchurch Road past the Sovereign Centre until you reach the end of the late 1980s pedestrianised precinct. Further on is an Art-Deco building (now **Motabitz**) on the right. This was originally the Gas & Water Company showroom (1933). Note the streamline curves and staircase tower.

Pause at the gates to **Woodland Walk**, with the Bournemouth coat of arms. *Pulchritudo et Salubritas* means 'Beauty and Health'. The Walk used to be the carriageway of Wentworth House, with **Portman Lodge** (now a funeral directors)

its lodge house. Wentworth was the summer residence of Lord Portman of Bryanston and was built *c* 1873, one of the first houses constructed from concrete. His estate adjoined Boscombe Manor

and extended to Fisherman's Walk. The house became Bournemouth Collegiate School in 1922 (see map). Portman Ravine was the house's beach access.

Take Woodland Walk and through trees on your left you will see the Roman Catholic **Church of Corpus Christi** (1895). Next to it is the **Anglo-European College of Chiropractic**, which occupies what was the Convent of the Cross, a Roman Catholic convent and school between 1887 and 1980.

Arriving at a pair of metal gateposts which once led to Wentworth House,

turn right onto Beechwood Avenue. **Shelley Manor** began as Boscombe Cottage, built in 1801 for Philip Norris, near the site of Boscombe Copperas House. In 1849 it became the home of Sir Percy Florence Shelley, who resided here for 40 years. The house was extended by Christopher Crabb Creeke and renamed Boscombe Manor in 1873. Sir Percy lived here until his death

in 1889 and Lady Shelley until her death 10 years later. The Shelleys' guests included writers R.L. Stevenson, Edward Trelawny, Leigh Hunt and Jefferson Hogg, politician Sir Henry Drummond Wolff, and actors Sir Henry Irving, Ellen Terry and Sir Beerbohm Tree. There is a blue plaque on the front of the building.

Turn left into Grovely Avenue and follow the path beside the tennis courts. Looking back, there is a good view of the modern apartments (left), the brick building which is the Grade II Listed **Shelley Theatre** (1870), with the rest of Shelley Manor now being the Medical Centre. Follow the path through **Shelley Park** to finish at Boscombe Overcliff Drive. The gardens were given by Lady Shelley and they contain an SSSI. There is a large marble sculpture of a dove, the idea of pupils of Avonbourne School, symbolising the despair and hope of Frankenstein. The sculptor, Andy Kirkby, also created Boscombe's Sea Road arts trail.

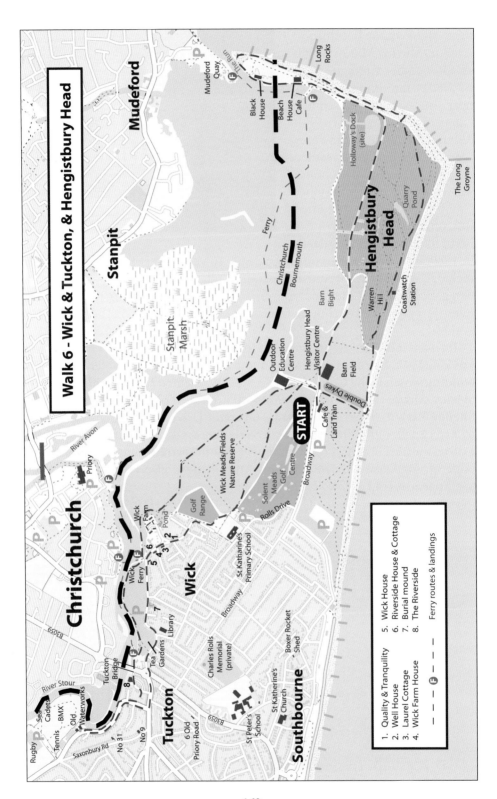

Walk 6 - Wick & Tuckton, & Hengistbury Head

Christchurch

Mudeford

Stanpit

Stanpit Marsh

River Avon

Priory

Wick Farm

Golf Range

Wick Meads/Fields Nature Reserve

Wick Pond

Wick

Wick Ferry

Library

Tea Gardens

Tuckton Bridge

River Stour

Old Waterworks

Tennis

BMX

Rugby

Sea Cadets

No 31

No 9

Saxonbury Rd

6 Old Priory Road

Tuckton

St Peter's School

St Katherine's Church

Charles Rolls Memorial (private)

St Katharine's Primary School

Boxer Rocket Shed

Southbourne

Broadway

Rolls Drive

Solent Meads Golf Centre

START

Cafe & Land Train

Broadway

Outdoor Education Centre

Hengistbury Head Visitor Centre

Barn Field

Double Dykes

Barn Bight

Warren Hill

Coastwatch Station

Hengistbury Head

Quarry Pond

Holloway's Dock (site)

The Long Groyne

Long Rocks

Cafe

Beach House

Black House

Mudeford Quay

The Run

Ferry

Christchurch Bournemouth

1. Quality & Tranquility
2. Well House
3. Laurel Cottage
4. Wick Farm House
5. Wick House
6. Riverside House & Cottage
7. Burial mound
8. The Riverside

Ferry routes & landings

B3059

162

Walk 6: Wick and Tuckton, and Hengistbury Head

This is a long walk, but as a figure of eight it can be tackled in two halves. It can also be shortened/eased by catching the land train and/or avoiding the walk out along Mudeford Sandbank.

> **Start and finish:** Hiker Cafe, Broadway, Bournemouth BH6 4EN
> **Approx. distance:** 13 km (two loops of 6.5 km each)

From the café, go to the end of Broadway road, then follow signs to Hengistbury Head Outdoor Adventure Centre. Just before the Centre there are two paths to the left with an information board. Take the wider left path between the golf course and nature reserve, then between the school and golf range, and into Wick Lane.

Head right along Wick Lane to **Wick Green**. The two whitewashed brick and slate properties to the right are named **Quality** (No. 2) and **Tranquility** (No. 4). The latter was briefly the village shop, selling ice creams and hot drinks, although the smell from the nearby piggery might have been off-putting! There was once an old village well and the **Well House** (No. 6) dates to 1908, with a barn at the rear where church services were once held.

Next on the left is **Wick House**, the local manor house, built *c* 1691, or later as some sources say it is Georgian; an extension (**Wick Cottage**) was certainly added later. Nelson reputedly dined at Wick House, and a subterranean passage allegedly led from here to Christchurch Priory crypt, one of the smugglers' many covert routes.

Towards the end of the Green on the left is **Laurel Cottage** (1851). On the corner with Branders Lane, **Wick Farm House** is a long, two-storey dwelling, originally the property of the lord of the manor, dating from at least 1770.

Across the road is **Riverside House**, and tucked behind it is 17th-century **Riverside Cottage**, the only thatched cottage in Wick today.

Take the solid path on the right, off the road, bending round Wick Lane. Further on, between Riversdale Road and Magnolia Close is a grassy mound which was found to be a **Bronze Age burial site**, showing the antiquity hereabouts.

Around the corner you come to **Tuckton Library**. This was built as Broom Close (1907/08) by architect Joseph Brewerton in the Arts and Crafts style, hence the rusticated Purbeck blocks and pebbledash. John King commissioned it, but never lived there as his wife disliked it!

At the roundabout, go straight on to Tuckton Road. Tuckton Farm used to be between Riverside Lane and Iford Lane (the farmhouse was demolished in 1930) and farm-workers' cottages existed in Riverside Lane, one of Bournemouth's oldest lanes, marked on 18th-century maps and probably used as a route for taking cattle to the Stour for watering (the Stour was known as Cows' River here).

Turn right into Iford Lane and continue until you see the building with a tall chimney. This is the **Old Waterworks**, built in 1857, which has a blue **plaque** commemorating that Count Vladimir Chertkov, a friend of Tolstoy, and fellow Russian emigres established 'The Free Age Press' here in 1897, and printed

Tolstoy's first works until 1908. The former pumping house had a steel-lined strong-room to store all the original Tolstoyan manuscripts. It was acquired by developers in 1988, who built several homes but incorporated the original arched facades to the front and Listed chimney to the rear.

In the late 19th century, the Russian émigré colony (see above) was housed nearby at **9 Saxonbury Road** (parallel with Iford Lane) in what used to be Tuckton House amid 10 acres of grounds. After the Russians moved out, the building became a nursing home, before being demolished in 1965 to make way for the current bungalow estate. **No. 31 Saxonbury Road** was built originally for Olga Tolstoy, the writer's daughter-in-law, sometime after May 1907. Artist Helen Constance Pym Sutton purchased the house in 1930, running art classes here throughout the 1930s; the house became a kindergarten in 1955 and has been a Montessori school since 2005. Novelist Salomé Hocking (1859–1927) lived at 6 Old Priory Road, Tuckton with her husband, publisher Arthur Fifield, who collaborated on the publication of Tolstoy's works.

Retrace your steps slightly and, if not too wet, take the **River Stour Walk** back along the riverbank. This pops back out again on Iford Lane. Turn left, then take FP117 (next left) to Riverside Lane, go left, then right through the pub car park.

The Riverside began life as the Terrace Tea Room (1920) and there was once a boat-house below the bridge. Today's **bridge** was built in 1905, enabling trams to cross to Christchurch (note the red plaque). At 347 ft long, it was the longest bridge of its type at the time, and the first such bridge to carry a tramway. It was a toll bridge until 1943, with a toll-house on the Christchurch side of the Stour, which survived to the mid-1950s.

Cross the road and walk down into **Tuckton Tea Gardens**, which began trading as Tuckton Creeks in 1903. Bournemouth Boating Services are based here and the ferries haul up here for maintenance during the off-season.

Keep walking along the riverside path until you reach **Wick Ferry**. You may see the ferry heading across the Stour to its other pontoon outside the Captain's Club Hotel & Spa. There has been some form of river crossing here for centuries, with the ferry between here and Tuckton commencing in 1814. It used to be a 'poled punt', also used by wildfowlers to shoot ducks. A motorized ferry wasn't introduced until 1947. Immediately after WWII, motor torpedo boats were moored along the south bank, converted into living accommodation because of the post-war housing crisis. These extended from Tuckton Bridge almost as far as the Wick Ferry.

Wick Ferry c 1913 (Wikimedia Commons) and Ferry Terminal c 1900 (Wikimedia Commons Queensland University of Technology. Digital Collections).

Continue along the footpath (this section can be flooded) back to Wick Lane, but then branch left to continue on the riverside path. After walking around the **Wick Farm** development (1985), glance back across the pond to the impressive house The Sanctuary, behind which is an older cottage with farm buildings, including a barn bearing the date 1846.

Enter the nature area of **Wick Fields and Reed Beds**. Follow the path, watching out for migratory birds, until you reach a wooden seat. This is one of several specially commissioned commemorative benches around the area carved by Tom Harvey using a chainsaw. Take the left path here. You will pass a bird-viewing platform, with handy apertures for humans of different heights. You might see song thrush, skylark, kestrel, barn owl and little owl, and rarer Dartford and Cetti's warblers. There can also be otters and water vole. A herd of Galloway cattle graze the land, as they are suited to harsher coastal and estuary conditions, and the grazing encourages wildflower meadows to grow, which in turn attracts rare bird and moth species.

Emerge by the entrance to the **Outdoor Education Centre**, run by Brockenhurst College, and turn right, back to the Hiker Cafe.

****

And now a walk round Hengistbury Head. First stop is the thatched **Visitor Centre**, which was officially opened in April 2014 by Chris Packham (see 'Nature Areas'). It has informative exhibits, webcams, and a wildlife garden and pond, so it's useful to visit before you go exploring the area. It is estimated Hengistbury Head has over one-million visitors annually.

Double back towards the car park and start walking along the fence on your left. This is protecting the **Double Dykes** ancient monument, a pair of banks and ditches dating to the Iron Age. At one point there is a recess in the fence allowing a closer look at the dykes. Around the 1890s, a bridge was thrown up between the two ditches for Army training purposes.

The large open field on the right is where Bournemouth's Centenary Air Pageant was held in 1910. Rolls Drive skirting the golf course recalls **Charles Rolls** (1877–1910), balloon and aviation enthusiast, and co-founder of Rolls-Royce. He was the second Briton to obtain a flying licence and the first man to fly across the Channel and back non-stop. Sadly, just over a month after this feat, he was also the first Briton to die in a powered flight, during the air show in 1910. He is commemorated by a stone memorial on the playing fields of St Peter's School, near the spot where his plane came down. Other aviators

Last flight of the Hon. C.S. Rolls, killed at Bournemouth when his biplane crashed from a height of around 100 ft. (Courtesy of Bournemouth Libraries.)

who flew at the Show were Claude Grahame-White, the first to make a night flight in April 1910, and Bertram Dickson, the first British serviceman to qualify as a pilot.

Continue to the end of the fence, then bear left around the southern end of the dykes. Follow the fence, climbing towards the sandstone headland (Warren Hill). On the way up there is a pond with an information board regarding the **natterjack toad**, reintroduced to the Head in 1989, having been absent since the 1950s.

On top of **Warren Hill** is a **trig point** which marks the Head's highest point (36 m a.s.l.) and toposcope (**orientation stone**). There are excellent views from here of Christchurch Harbour and its entrance (the Run). The Head forms the southern boundary of the harbour, a natural breakwater protecting it from prevailing south-westerlies. Looking back the way you walked up, note the narrow part of the Head between the sea and small harbour inlet known as Barn Bight, the area considered most at risk of a breach. If the sea overwhelmed this low area, the Head could become an island, threatening both Christchurch and its harbour. Late in the 20th century, erosion of the southern cliff face (left) was as rapid as 1.2 m (4 ft) a year, resulting in a Shoreline Management Plan, with beaches replenished with sand and shingle since the 1990s.

Walk on to the **National Coastwatch station**. In the late 18th century there were two structures here: a summer-house built by Gustavus Brander, a former governor of the Bank of England, which was demolished by 1843, and a coastal lookout/signal house. One of the wrecks that would

have been witnessed from here was the *Good Intent*, which ran aground off the Double Dykes in 1809, with 100 troops aboard returning from the Battle of Corunna, all surviving. The current building remained a coastguard lookout station until the mid-1990s; it then lay abandoned until August 2018, when it was taken over by the National Coastwatch Institution, which is now manning it from a pool of around 100 volunteer watchkeepers. It operates 364 days a year during daylight hours, and there's a Friends of Hengistbury Head Lookout (www.hhnci.org.uk/friends).

Continue walking over the hill. When you reach a fork, bear right to **Quarry Pond**. This pond is one happy legacy of the Hengistbury Mining Company (1840–80), which took ironstone 'doggers' (boulders) from the quarries here, the beach and reef – a triple whammy as it wasn't appreciated at the time how damaging this was to the Head's stability.

Follow the path to the end of the Head, where there is a **viewpoint**, before descending steps to the beach, emerging at the beginning of the **beach huts**. The first huts were erected here in 1929 and there are now about 350 of the country's most expensive (one sold in July 2018 for £300,000), strung out along Mudeford Spit.

You now have the option of walking out along the **Spit**. The beach here was named the fourth best in the UK in March 2014. At the end is the **Black House**, erected in the 1750s. It was a centre for shipbuilding, with several ships over 100 tons being built while propped up against the right-hand wall, a sail loft and accommodation for boat-builders. It was also reputedly used by smugglers who hauled contraband over the Head and concealed some of their kegs in the Double Dykes. Between 1880 and 1935 a build-up of sand created a mile-long channel out of the harbour all the way to Highcliffe Castle beach, until a storm removed it. The Spit is also the end of the 64-mile-long Stour Valley Way.

Head back, along the other (harbour) side of the Spit, passing the jetty for **ferries** to Mudeford Quay, Christchurch Town Quay, Wick Ferry and Tuckton Tea Gardens, and the **Beach House Café**.

At the **Lagoon and Holloway's Dock**, ironstone doggers, mined in the 19th century, were once loaded onto barges for the blast furnaces of Merthyr Tydfil and the Rhondda Valley.

If operating, you can take the land train from here; if not, it's a sheltered walk back. As you come within sight of the Visitor Centre, beside Barn Bight you'll see some of the **doggers** along the roadway.

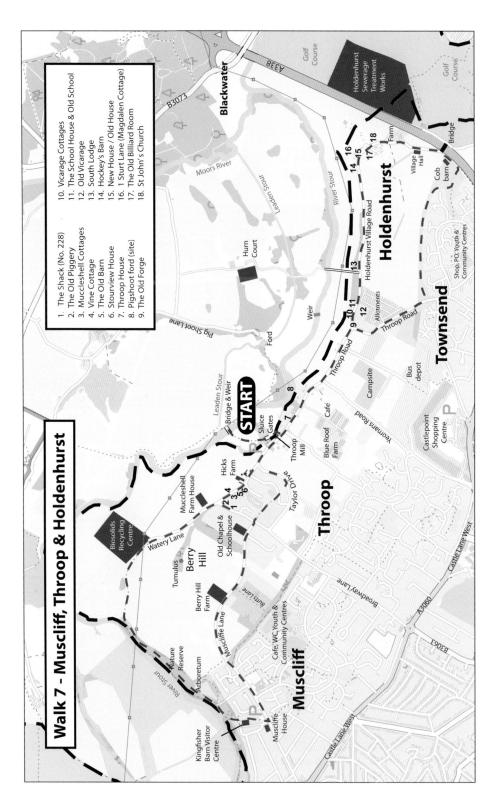

Walk 7 - Muscliff, Throop & Holdenhurst

1. The Shack (No. 228)
2. The Old Piggery
3. Muccleshell Cottages
4. Vine Cottage
5. The Old Barn
6. Stourview House
7. Throop House
8. Pigshoot ford (site)
9. The Old Forge
10. Vicarage Cottages
11. The School House & Old School
12. Old Vicarage
13. South Lodge
14. Hockey's Barn
15. New House / Old House
16. 1 Sturt Lane (Magdalen Cottage)
17. The Old Billiard Room
18. St John's Church

Walk 7: Muscliff, Throop and Holdenhurst

This figure-of-eight walk affords a glimpse of farming communities that pre-date the establishment of 'modern' Bournemouth.

Start and finish: Throop Mill, Throop Road, BH8 0DL
Approx. distance: 10 km (two loops of 5 km each)
Safety note: There are some on-road sections to this walk as the country lanes generally don't have pavements.

From Throop Mill walk west along Throop Road (there is no pavement, but it's a relatively quiet lane). Turn left into Taylor Drive and after about 200 m take Lavender Walk between the houses. There is a **pretty green and pond**, but you continue on across an open field until you meet Broadway Lane.

Go straight across into Muscliffe Lane. On your right is **The Old Chapel and Schoolhouse**. The chapel (1828) was built as the Independent Chapel, becoming Throop Congregational Church, then Throop United Reformed Church. A schoolroom was added at the back in 1830 and services

were announced by hoisting a large white flag and use of a speaking-trumpet. The chapel closed in 2010 due to contraction of the URC.

Continue along Muscliffe Lane and just before the priority traffic sign, the line of tall trees to the left marks former Butts Lane, an old track to Castle Lane. There are several farms and smallholdings along Muscliffe Lane, including **Berry Hill Farm** which sells seasonal vegetables. Seven pairs of semi-detached smallholders' dwellings were built (1920) here as part of the 'Homes for Heroes' land settlement programme after WWI.

Carry on through the encroaching conurbation until you reach Granby Road car park. The large white house on the corner is **Muscliff House**, a late-18th-century farmhouse.

Behind the car park is **Kingfisher Barn Visitor Centre**, opened in May 2016 and the focal point of the Stour Valley Nature Reserve. The 'Kingfisher' is apt as

you might see one diving into the river to feed.

Walk down to the river and turn right. After 50 m take the short flight of steps up into **Muscliff Arboretum**. As of 2014 there were 80 specimen trees. The Field of Hope (1993) is a riot of daffodils in spring and was planted in association with Marie Curie.

Head out of the north-west corner of the arboretum to rejoin the riverside path, which skirts along the side of the **Nature Reserve**. Eventually the path bears right, with Berry Hill to your right.

After passing the Biosolids Recycling Centre, proceed along Watery Lane. A Red Arrows Hawk T1 jet crashed just north of here during the August 2011 Bournemouth Air Festival, resulting in the tragic loss of the pilot Flt Lt Jon Egging.

Muccleshell Farmhouse on the left, once known as Muccleshell Hall, is believed to be the oldest complete structure in Bournemouth, with parts dating back to 1587, when it was thatched (it is believed the roof

was slated in 1729). One legend associated with it is that Charles II hid here for a night, presumably after his defeat at the Battle of Worcester in 1651 which led to his fleeing the country. In 1920 it was announced that the farm would become smallholdings for unemployed ex-servicemen following WWI.

Arriving at the junction of Throop Road and Broadway Lane, the curved building facing you is **The Old Piggery**. Take a slight detour right to see **The Shack** (No. 228), which is a late-17th-century Grade II Listed brick farmhouse and not like any shack I've ever seen. It is thatched and whitewashed, and has picturesque leaded windows of that era.

Return to the Piggery junction and bear right, around the bend into Throop Road, past **Muccleshell Cottages** on the right, another evocation of the lost village of Muccleshell (see 'Some Outlying Areas of the Borough').

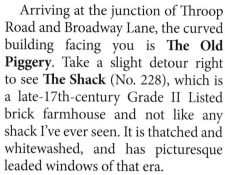

Vine Cottage (left), which looks early 19th century, was once owned by Rev. F. Hopkins, the first vicar of Holdenhurst. **The Old Barn** (right) is immediately followed by **Stourview House**, which dates to around 1790 and has a Georgian porch supported by slender columns. This was once the home of a maltster and ships' biscuit-maker, said to have been supplying the Navy, including *HMS Victory*, at the time of Nelson and Trafalgar.

Hicks Farm (left) and **River Farm** (almost opposite the mill) remind us of the essentially agricultural nature of this landscape. Although looking rather neglected (2019), there are plans to rejuvenate the Hicks Farm site as part of the Stour Valley Masterplan (2013), building on the success of Kingfisher Barn and hoping to emulate some of the popularity of Hengistbury Head Visitor Centre.

Back at the car park, **Throop Mill** has been derelict since 1974 but has a lengthy history. It is believed a mill of some sort has existed here since the

11th century. Some sources claim the present mill dates back to at least the 16th century, while others claim it was built around the mid-19th century. It alternated between grinding corn and grist (malt). The mill still bears the indistinct name of Parsons & Sons, the last family who operated it. It was water-powered until 1939, when a diesel engine was installed, before switching to electricity in 1960. A footpath behind leads across the mill stream sluices to the **weir** on the main river.

Just after the mill is **Throop House**, which dates to 1807 and stands on raised ground. This was the home of Sylvia, Dowager Countess of Malmesbury, between 1929 and 1939.

Refreshments are sparse on this walk, so you may wish to visit the 'C U Latte' portacabin **café** on the Blue Roof Farm/Throop Business Park. The nearby bungalow actually has a blue roof!

Back to Throop Road and directly opposite is **Pig Shoot**, the name coming from 'shute' or 'chute', dating to Saxon times, denoting a piece of muddy land detached from the main settlement only suitable for pigs. The site of **Pigshoot Ford** can be seen down the track on the right-hand side of the property, across which Sir Walter Tyrrell is said to have fled after firing the arrow that killed William II (Rufus). Its structure was deliberately weakened during WWII and it washed away, but there is still a lengthy ford across the Leaden Stour opposite on Pig Shoot Lane (see map). Both fords were reputedly used by smugglers. The next house along is aptly named **Deep Ford**.

You may have started to notice the ornate lamp-posts, still with their gas wicks, and operated by a clockwork mechanism to turn on the gas. There are 28 in the Throop and Holdenhurst area. These were installed between 1902 and 1910 by Christchurch Borough Council (Holdenhurst did not become part of Bournemouth until 1931), with the posts made from cast iron by Ringwood and Pokesdown Foundries. They were due to be replaced by the local electricity company that was converting gas lamps in Bournemouth, but Throop and Holdenhurst were inexplicably forgotten!

At the junction with Holdenhurst Village Road, bear left. Note **The Old Forge** on your right; this former smithy closed in the 1930s, as vehicles replaced horses, and the building was used as the village post office for some years, before being modernised as a private house.

The delightful terrace of **Vicarage Cottages** is on the left, followed by **The Schoolhouse** and **The Old School**, built around 1846, which hasn't echoed to the sound of tiny feet since about 1948. Behind the wall on the right is **The Old Vicarage**, built in 1883 by Rev. F. Hopkins, which later became a hotel and is now a private residence. Its significant **Coach House** is now a separate property, round the corner on Throop Road.

You then reach **South Lodge** and the private drive to Hurn Court. *Hurn* means a bend in the river in Old English. **Hurn Court**, or Heron Court as it was known until 1935, was the seat of the Earls of Malmesbury, chief landowners in Holdenhurst from 1795 until 1950, before becoming a boys' boarding school in 1952. This once grand house has now been converted into apartments. During the 3rd Earl's tenure, Benjamin Disraeli was a regular visitor. Disraeli held some Cabinet meetings at the Bath Hotel in Bournemouth and Malmesbury was his Lord Privy Seal. The house also appears in Thomas Hardy's novels as Rookington House.

Continue 500 m, along the lane. **Hockeys Barn** on your left marks the entrance to Holdenhurst village. Facing the green is **The New House** (late 17th century), thought to have been built by William Clapcott, a Wimborne banker. Attached is **The Old House** (early 17th century) which is thatched and once had some of its small back windows removed, indicating it was built before 1697 when a window tax on houses with over six windows resulted in them being blocked up to avoid paying tax.

Detour left into Sturt Lane to see **Magdalen Cottage** (No. 1), the cutest of low thatched cottages. It is said to be the village's oldest surviving building and gets its name from ancient links to the Magdalen Charity that ran the leper hospital at Christchurch and rented out the cottage to help fund the hospital. It is of timber frame construction, with later brick infilling. The

door is believed to be that from the old Saxon church (now replaced by St John's), purchased in 1764 for 2s. There are unusual carvings on the outside of the building (which aren't possible to see), one of a grotesque (emaciated) head, the other of a human chest with ribs revealed.

At the end of the lane is a peaceful **green area**, the resting place of Pincher, Laddie and Snatcher. You can also see the raised bank that seems to protect the village from the river. Retrace your steps back to the centuries-old village green where fêtes are still held. On the right-hand-side is **The Old Billiard Room**, which might have been about all the entertainment there was in Holdenhurst in days past.

Beyond the green is the church of **St John**. The previous old church was mentioned in *Domesday Book* and, in a bad state of repair by the early 19th century, was replaced by today's version in 1834. The land was donated by

First Baron Sir George Ivison Tapps (1753–1835), Lord of the Manor of Christchurch. The Norman font from the old church has pride of place, and the church has an elegant turret at its west end. The Lych Gate and War Memorial are worth a look too.

Walk on past **Holdenhurst Farm**, one of the few working farms left in the borough, and the village hall. Just past the bridge is an old **cob barn/ fuel house** with a corrugated tin roof, all that remains of Townsend Cottages, which were destroyed in a fire. At around 500 years old, it is one of the very earliest remaining buildings. Cob is clay mixed with straw, gravel and sand. The gates just beyond the barn were used to allow cattle to be taken across the earlier and much quieter versions of the A338, with traffic lights halting the cars!

This whole area is due significant change as part of the A338 Wessex Fields link junction plan. An entrance is being created into a new business park behind the Royal Bournemouth Hospital. The footbridge may be replaced by a vehicular and pedestrian flyover/junction. Although no immediate further threat, this area may also be considered as a route for a Castle Lane relief road.

Take the path on the right past a BMX track, crossing the playing fields to the right and skirting the back of the houses along a grassy track. Turn right on Throop Road. There are glimpses of the back of Castlepoint Shopping Centre away to the left. After passing **Longbarrow Allotments** you are back at the junction next to The Old Forge. Turn left and head back to Throop Mill.

Other Walks and Cycling Routes

The **Stour Valley Way** is a designated long-distance footpath following almost all the 64-mile course of the river, from Stourhead to Hengistbury Head. Bournemouth has some beautiful sections, including between Tuckton Bridge and Hengistbury Head, and along Riverside Avenue (it's possible to walk from Holdenhurst village (Walk 7), crossing the A338 Spur Road on a footbridge, then following Riverside Avenue alongside Iford Golf Centre, down to Iford, seeing the Stour's limit of navigation along the way). There are also walks from Throop Mill and Kingfisher Barn Visitor Centre (both featured in Walk 7), with plans to link these up with Hengistbury Head as part of a new 'Stour Valley Park'.

The self-guided 3.5-mile **Stream, Heath and Woodland Walk** can be downloaded from Bournemouth Tourism's website (https://www.bournemouth.co.uk/things-to-do/activities/walking-and-hiking). It starts from the Cenotaph and takes in the Central and Upper Gardens, Coy Pond, Talbot Heath, Pug's Hole and Meyrick Park.

Meyrick Park has three walking routes: Meyrick Trail (1.5 miles), Tapps Trail (1.25 miles) and the Cross Country Jogging Trail (2.4 miles).

The council runs a range of **Guided Walks and Monday Morning Meanders** with different routes throughout the year. They usually last between 1 and 2 hours. A charge may apply for the guided walks, but the Meanders are free. The latter stroll through some of the borough's most beautiful countryside.

Bournemouth Tree Trail highlights 14 tree species to be found in the Central and Upper Gardens, including Redwood, Cypress, Palm, Cedar, Walnut, Wellingtonia, London Plane, Birch and Oak. There's also a Horse Chestnut near the War Memorial planted in the reign of Queen Victoria. The Trail is free, well signed and takes around 2 hours. There is a free trail leaflet, including map, available online and locally.

Bourne Valley Greenway is a 4-mile cycling/walking route between Bournemouth Pier and Gravel Hill in Poole. It runs across Canford Heath and follows the stream through Bourne Bottom, across Talbot Heath, past The Greenway at Scott Road, Wallisdown, Coy Pond and into Bournemouth Gardens. It's popular with locals using it to reach the town centre, commuters and school children. It also encourages visitors to explore out of town.

Bournemouth Coast Path is a 37-mile long-distance walk that connects the Dorset Coast Path with the Solent Way. It stretches from Swanage to Lymington, including nature reserves at Studland (Isle of Purbeck), Hengistbury Head and Keyhaven Marshes (Hampshire).

Walkingtalks was started by Hattie Miles, who was born and brought up in Kent but moved to Bournemouth in 1986 to work as a photographer for a new weekly newspaper, the *Bournemouth Express*. She became the first woman photographer on the then-*Evening Echo*. Today, Hattie still works as a freelance photographer.

'My first love is photography, but I also enjoy writing, so enjoy combining the two on my guided walks. The first walk I came up with was Wonderful Westbourne. I now have half-a-dozen different Bournemouth walks, including Hidden Secrets, Romance & Scandal, and the new Darker Side. I also have The Language of Colour, a lovely Autumn walk, where we enjoy the seasonal hues and discuss how writers have used language over the years to describe the different colours. I'm also able to use anecdotal stories from my time working as a photojournalist – I believe it adds real human interest when I can say "So and so told me ..." or "I was there". My walks are usually combined with the opportunity for a pleasant refreshments stop either before or after (or both!).' (www.walkingtalks. wordpress.com)

Bournemouth beach has a fabulous promenade for **cycling**, extending along Sandbanks as far as Poole (west) and Hengistbury Head (east). It is not permissible to cycle on the prom between 10am and 6pm in July and August due to the large number of pedestrians, although this restriction does not apply between Bournemouth and Boscombe piers. There are non-vehicular cycle paths at Hengistbury Head.

For more cycling ideas check out the Area Cycle Map published by Bournemouth Tourism.

Some Outlying Areas of the Borough

Boscombe and Springbourne

Boscombe was once separated from Bournemouth by heathland and was known as Boscomb until the 19th century (the name could come from *bos*, Cornish for house, and *cumb*, Old English for narrow valley). It provided artisans (skilled workmen) that the new, genteel watering hole of Bournemouth required. Boscombe became part of Bournemouth in 1876. See Walk 5.

Springbourne is sandwiched between the A338 Wessex Way and railway line, and was once known as Boscombe Heath. It too began as an area for artisans working in Bournemouth, and many of the Victorian cottages they lived in can still be seen today near Holdenhurst Road. The Cricketers Arms in Windham Road is said to be the oldest pub in Bournemouth, with its original stables and coach house. Springbourne Library opened in 1909 and is a Carnegie library (one of 2,509 libraries built around the world with money donated by philanthropist Andrew Carnegie).

Charminster, Strouden Park and Queens Park

In 1841, just three families were listed in the Charminster census, and the first modern dwellings were not built until around 1880, when Edward Harris, 4th Earl of Malmesbury, allowed building on land he owned here. With Malmesbury Park Estate came the Catholic Church of the Annunciation (finished 1907), designed by Giles Gilbert Scott and George Bodley. Charminster is notable for having two blue plaques in one street, commemorating two recipients of the Victoria Cross killed during WWI. No. 39 Capstone Road was the home of Frederick Charles Riggs, killed in action on 1 October 1918 (the house has been demolished, so the plaque is on No. 45). There is a memorial to him at Malmesbury Park School. No. 175 was the home of Cecil Reginald Noble, who was fatally wounded on 12 March 1915.

Cecil Reginald Noble VC.

Further building took place during the 1920s, which also resulted in the opening of Charminster Library (1932) designed by Frederick Dolamore (of first beach-hut fame). Famous residents of Charminster have included the Durrells, who owned two homes in St Albans Avenue after they departed Corfu in 1939 (see 'The Arts').

Strouden Park includes Castlepoint shopping centre (on the former site of Strouden Park Hotel (1932–2001)) and Yeoman's Road retail park, plus Townsend Estate, which has its own community centre in Jewell Road and a community garden that has won a Green Pennant Award. Strouden Park Community Centre has been in existence since 1987, but opened its new building in Vanguard Road in 2012.

Queens Park includes one of Bournemouth's largest parks (see 'Nature Areas').

Iford and Tuckton – see Walk 6

Iford, Tuckton and Wick all border the River Stour as it heads south and east into Christchurch Harbour. Iford dates to Anglo-Saxon times, its name coming from Saxon words *ea* and *ford* denoting a shallow place in a river. Up to the 20th century it was still an attractive hamlet of just a few thatched cottages. There was originally a ford over the Stour, with the old Iford Bridge dating back to at least the 12th century. Today's old bridge, used by pedestrians, consists of several sections, including the Great Bridge dating to 1784. With increased motor traffic, a new bridge was needed, so the new £60,000 Iford Bridge was built in 1933, but, fortunately, with the old bridge preserved.

As previously mentioned, there was a Russian presence at Tuckton House on Saxonbury Road, where an émigré colony, fleeing Tsarist oppression, set up camp in 1900, to print and disseminate the works of Leo Tolstoy, using an old water-pumping station. One employee, Alexander Sirnis, would father a daughter, Melita Norwood (1912–2005), who later spent 40 years passing Anglo-American atomic bomb secrets to the KGB, before being unmasked in 1999. She was born in Bournemouth and died in Pokesdown, aged 93. The film *Red Joan* (2018) is based on her life, starring Sophie Cookson and Dame Judi Dench.

A ford existed at Tuckton prior to a bridge, hence the hamlet's old name of Tuckford, and there was a ferry service between 1800 and 1880. Before the Tuckton Bridge, it was quite a journey up stream to the old Iford Bridge.

Old Iford Bridge, with three distinctly different sections.

Tuckton had a wooden bridge from 1881, replaced with a ferro-concrete one in 1905 when the tramway extended to Christchurch. There was a toll house on the Christchurch side, with tolls only ceasing in 1943 (the ending of tolls presumably hastened by the opening of the new Iford Bridge 10 years before).

Kinson

Kinson appears in *Domesday Book* but is most famous for its smuggling past. Gulliver's Tavern had been a landmark pub on the main Wimborne Road since the mid-19th century, recalling Isaac Gulliver, the doyen of local smugglers. It recently reopened as the Acorn Pub and has a wealth of smuggling history, and hauntings. There may have been a church on the St Andrew's Church, Millhams Road site since Saxon times (*c* 950 AD). The *c* 1100 AD Norman tower is believed to be the oldest part of the existing building. The chancel was rebuilt in 1875, but the chancel arch dates back to at least 1300 AD. It has smugglers' graves, including that of Robert Trotman, shot dead by customs men in 1765. The tower was used for storing contraband. The present church was rebuilt in 1895.

Pelhams Park also lies on Millhams Road,

St Andrew's Church, Kinson.

with Kinson Community Centre at his heart. Kinson Manor Farmhouse (or Kinson Farm), Manor Farm Road, dates back to *c* 1700. Kinson joined Bournemouth in 1931. The village green was established in 1968.

Littledown

For centuries Littledown was a small heathland farming settlement, south of the much more important Holdenhurst village. As Bournemouth expanded, Littledown remained a farming community, with the Cooper-Dean family residing in Littledown House up on the ridge. In the early 1980s the last descendants, two spinster sisters, sold up to Bournemouth Council and much of the land was sold off for housing, but with a large section set by for a park and sports centre. Notable buildings today include the JP Morgan Chase bank campus with approximately 4,000 employees, Royal Bournemouth Hospital with about 900 staff, Bournemouth County Court, Littledown Leisure Centre, the Village Hotel, and a home for retired nurses.

Littledown House – on private land, but just visible from the mini railway.

The 18th-century Grade II listed Littledown House is located on the private JP Morgan Bank campus and has been well restored. As there were no heirs to the estate, the Alice Ellen Cooper-Dean Foundation was established for 'relief of poverty, distress, and sickness, the advancement of education and religion and other charitable purposes of benefit to the community'. Grants are available for registered charities in Dorset and West Hampshire and many international projects.

Until recently there were still signs of a former traffic lights and cattle crossing over the busy A338 Spur Road. When first built, this road cut off the Cooper-Deans' land at Littledown from their farms at Holdenhurst, and the crossing was a concession to the family.

Muscliff, Throop and Holdenhurst – see Walk 7

Muscliff (or Muscliffe) comes from the Old English meaning 'cliff inhabited by mice'. On the gentle slopes of Berry Hill (private land) there is a Bronze Age tumulus. Bronze Age urns have been found at Sandringham Gardens and Cheddington Road.

The name of Muccleshell Farm in Throop recalls a lost village, Muccleshell, which had a population of around 120 in the early 1840s but was swallowed up by neighbouring Throop. *Muccleshell* could derive from Muckles Hill, an alternative name for Berry Hill, *muckel* meaning much or big (though Berry Hill isn't much of a hill today).

Fishing must have been an important source of food in the hamlets strung out along the Stour in times past. Throop Fisheries is run by Ringwood & District Angling Association, and day-tickets can be obtained to fish over 5 miles of river plus side streams, offering some of the best river fishing in the South. Species include barbel, chub, carp, roach, tench, perch, dace, pike, and bream.

Holdenhurst has had several name changes over the centuries. It was originally *Holeest*, from Old English *holegn* (holly) and *hyrst* (copse), and is mentioned in *Domesday Book*, along with Throop Mill (holly still grows extensively here particularly along Holdenhurst Road). It is regarded as Bournemouth's mother village, and sometimes the 'forgotten village'. Holdenhurst Road would originally have been the main road into Bournemouth from the north (now it's the A338 Wessex Way). The village is quiet, as it is a no-through road, but the noise from the A338 is ever present. However, the rural atmosphere is preserved and it is hard to imagine we are on the outskirts of Bournemouth.

Ensbury and Redhill

Ensbury was an ancient village adjoining Kinson, and was mainly farmland up to the 1930s. Although Ensbury Manor was demolished, its Grade II Listed former dower house survives at 1300 Wimborne Road, and the Old Vicarage (1785) for St Andrew's is today a Toby Carvery in Northbourne. Talbot Woods flying school was moved to Ensbury Park in 1917, becoming a civilian aerodrome in 1919 (offering passenger flights and tuition). Air races and greyhound and horse racing were held here in the 1920s, but a series of mishaps led to its closure in 1928, and by 1932 the racecourse cum aerodrome was being redeveloped for housing.

There was once a tea garden and ferry crossing the River Stour at Redhill, at the bottom of Redhill Drive across the other side of today's Whitelegg Way, where Wheatplot Residential Park is. The ferry closed in 1934. The Horse and Jockey pub (1841) on Wimborne Road must have been busy with ferry patrons. The name recalls the nearby Ensbury Park racecourse, which operated in the 1920s. The pub became the Smoking Outlaw in 2016 before closing. At the bottom of Redhill Drive/Avenue is Redhill Park/Common, with a cafe and play area (see Gardens and Nature Areas).

Pokesdown

Pokesdown lies between Boscombe and Southbourne in eastern Bournemouth. Although there is evidence of human habitation going back to the Bronze Age, modern Pokesdown really dates to the late 18th/early 19th century, when it developed just to the west of Stourfield House. Some believe 'Pokesdown' is derived from Puck's Down, or Pixie's Down. It sounds like the 'little people' may have been in the vicinity!

Pokesdown Congregational Church (1858) at the junction of Southbourne Road and Stourvale Road was one of Bournemouth's oldest places of worship. It is now a very spacious two-bedroom house.  St James' (also 1858) on Christchurch Road is a beautiful sandstone church designed by George Edmund Street, with a lovely interior including Purbeck marble adornments.

Pokesdown Congregational Church

Pokesdown has the only extant railway station in the borough, other than Bournemouth. It opened in 1886 and was rebuilt in the early 1930s. East Cemetery, north of the station, opened in 1897. Pokesdown was another area that started as an artisans' quarter, before joining Bournemouth in 1901.

Southbourne

As part of the Stourfield Chase hunting estate, Edmund Bott built Stourfield House in 1766 on high ground overlooking the Stour valley in the area of heath known as Southbourne. It was renamed Douglas House, became a hospital, and was demolished in 1990.

The area once had pretensions as a watering-hole of its own. Dr T.A. Compton bought 230 acres of land for £3,000 in 1870, optimistically naming it Southbourne-on-Sea. By 1874 Southbourne had its own Winter Gardens and in 1888 a

The original staircase and portico from Stourfield House, here incorporated into Douglas Mews flats, built in 1993.

Fisherman's Walk Cliff Lift opened in 1935.

pier. Alas, its ill-fated pier scheme ended in failure, as did its Undercliff Esplanade, though the cliff lift is still operational. St Katharine's Church on Church Road owes its dedication to Dr Compton, who appreciated the closeness of St Catherine's Hill (Christchurch) and St Catherine's Point (Isle of Wight).

Southbourne became part of Bournemouth in 1901. Bournemouth Corporation's first housing scheme was Carbery Estate in West Southbourne (1920). The Shell Garden at 137 Overcliff Drive was a popular attraction between 1948 and 2001.

Talbot Woods

Talbot Woods gets its name from the large plantation of pine trees that once covered the area. Old Talbot village, built between 1850 and 1862, was the brainchild of two benevolent sisters, Georgina and Mary Talbot, who employed poor labourers to clear the land and build cottages for themselves in a 'model village' environment. Several alms houses were built, designed by Christopher Crabb Creeke, with a school added in 1862. St Mark's Church dates to 1870. There were half-a-dozen farms providing employment and trade. Bournemouth University now occupies much of the land that once belonged to Talbot Village Farm. There was also a flying training school here preparing pilots during WWI (1915–17), after which it moved to Ensbury Park (above). The original Talbot Woods airfield was used again briefly in WWII (May–June 1944).

Westbourne – see Walk 4

Wick and Hengistbury Head – see Walk 6

The original name of the hamlet of Wick was Wic (Old English for village or dairy farm), dating to around 1100, and it has had various spellings since. It remains a quiet backwater, unlike Iford and Tuckton, which seem more swallowed up. Wick has a long-established ferry crossing the Stour to Christchurch, with some historians believing the ferry rights date back before the Priory. There is certainly no doubt the ferry has been operating for 200–250 years. It runs every day between April and October, tide and weather permitting.

Hengistbury Head was inhabited as long ago as the New Stone Age and was an important fortified port during the Iron Age. It ceased to be a centre of population sometime after the Roman invasion, as the Romans established their own ports and towns. It was first referred to as *Hednesburia* in the 12th century, but adopted its current spelling in the 18th/19th centuries, possibly because it was believed the legendary Anglo-Saxon leader Hengist was buried on the Head (though there is no evidence he was).

Hengistbury Head could have looked very different today had any of several schemes for the area materialised. Back in the 1600s, Andrew Yarranton, sponsored by Edward Hyde, the Earl of Clarendon, Lord of the Manor of Christchurch and Chancellor to Charles II, planned a naval gunnery foundry, dockyard and fort here. Because of the difficulty navigating the harbour entrance (The Run), a cutting was made through the spit near today's café. It

was built by 1698 and in operation for up to 30 years; however, the jetty built on the north side failed to protect it from prevailing winds and the cutting often silted up because of longshore drift. Remains of the 'Clarendon Jetty', also known as Long Rocks, are still visible at low tide halfway along the spit.

In the 1700s, famous lighthouse builder John Smeaton proposed a canal through the spit and a southern jetty to protect it. Then in 1885, Christchurch & Wimborne Railway Company proposed a 1000-yard breakwater protecting the harbour entrance, a major dock and railway back to Wimborne. And finally, Harry Selfridge, while leasing Highcliffe Castle (1916–22), purchased the Head with the intention of building the largest castle in the world. With his spending power reduced after the Wall Street Crash, he sold the area to Bournemouth Council in May 1930, for £25,250, with the handy proviso the land would never be built on.

Winton and Moordown

Winton was once a distinct area, separated from Bournemouth by rough, undeveloped land. It began as a region for artisans, becoming part of the

View from Hengistbury Head along Mudeford Spit (also known as Mudeford Sandbank, Mudeford Beach or 'The Island').

borough in 1901 and receiving its first trams in 1903. In the same year, author Flora Thompson came to live here, making use of Winton Library which opened in 1907. Also in that year, Winton played its part in Robert Baden-Powell's first scout camp, when seven teenage members of the Winton Boys' Brigade were among the full complement of 20-odd, from different backgrounds, who headed to Brownsea Island in Poole Harbour. The name Winton originates from the Earl of Winton, a Scottish kinsman of the Talbot sisters, who named roads in the area after Scottish towns and people.

Moordown began as a mainly agricultural community, which by the end of the 19th century was regarded as a hamlet within the parish of Winton (above), which had been expanding rapidly. Moordown also began to grow after Winton and itself became part of Bournemouth in 1901. The corner of Wimborne Road and Malvern Road once had a tramway depot (1906), marking the end of the northern tram route. Mayfield Park Estate was typical of Moordown's growth-spurt, being laid out to mark the coronation of George V (June 1911), hence King Edward Avenue (his predecessor), King George Avenue and Queen Mary Avenue (his queen, Mary of Teck).

Help and Information

Maps

The general area is covered by OS Explorer map OL22 and Landranger 195. A detailed map of the town is available from the Bournemouth Tourist Information Centre.

Tourist Information Centre

Pier Approach,
Bournemouth,
Dorset, BH2 5AA,
tel 01202 451781
Open daily (except Christmas
Day) 9 am until 4 pm Jan–Mar
and Nov–Dec, 5 pm Apr–Jun and
Sep–Oct, and 6 pm Jul–Aug.

Transport

Wilts & Dorset (tel 0845 0727 093) and Yellow Buses (tel 01202 636110) operate frequent services to and from Bournemouth, with many services beginning and ending in Gervis Place near The Square.

Trains leave from the main station in Holdenhurst Road, plus Pokesdown station. There are three trains an hour to London (Waterloo), operated by South Western Railway, including a fast-service, which does not stop at Pokesdown. There is also a service to Poole, Dorchester and Weymouth. There is an hourly service to and from Manchester (Bournemouth only) which is operated by Virgin. The main station forms part of a travel interchange where local bus services and National Express coaches are also available, offering frequent services to London, and Heathrow and Gatwick airports. Taxis pick up at the main station.

Bournemouth Airport (originally named RAF Hurn) is situated in Christchurch, offering flights to over nine countries, principally with Ryanair and TUI. New routes for 2019 were Dublin, Prague and Paphos.

Russell-Cotes Art Gallery and Museum

East Cliff Promenade, tel 01202 451858
Open 10 am–5 pm Tue–Sun and Bank Holiday Mondays.
Closed Mondays, Good Friday, Christmas Day and Boxing Day.

As well as the beautiful rooms of the house, there are four purpose-built galleries where many of the largest works of the founding art collection are displayed. Other rooms include the Mikado's Room, devoted to the Russell-Cotes' Japanese collection; the Boudoir, which was Annie's private room, where she took tea with Princess Beatrice when the first three galleries were formally opened in February 1919; and the Irving Room, devoted to the Russell-Cotes' friend, theatre impresario Sir Henry Irving. There is a collection of porcelain and furniture, and the picture collection includes such artists as Sir Edwin Landseer, David Cox and Jean-Honoré Fragonard. The garden is a delight with its Victorian stone grotto and fountain and Japanese garden. There is also a café and shop.

Bournemouth Library

22, The Triangle, tel 01202 454848
Open 9:30 am Tue–Fri, 10 am Mon and Sat.
Closed 7 pm Mon–Thu, 5 pm Fri–Sat.

There are additional libraries in Boscombe (Hawkwood Road), at Castlepoint (Castle Lane West), Charminster (Strouden Avenue), Ensbury Park (Columbia Road), Kinson Hub (Wimborne Road), Pokesdown and Southbourne (Seabourne Road), Springbourne (Holdenhurst Road), Tuckton (Wick Lane), West Howe (Cunningham Crescent), Westbourne (Alum Chine Road) and Winton (Wimborne Road).

Lifeguards

RNLI lifeguards patrol the beach between May and September, with ten lifeguard stations between Alum Chine and Southbourne.

Bournemouth's Plaques

The following is a list of the borough's plaques. All plaques are of the round blue type unless stated otherwise. A free illustrated information leaflet about the blue plaques, produced by Bournemouth Borough Council, can be downloaded online.

Walk 1

Aubrey Beardsley (Green plaque)	Exeter Road
Bournemouth Centenary 1990 (Green plaque)	Iron Pergola, Central Gardens
Court Royal (Guglielmo Marconi)	Court Royal, South Cliff Road
Freddie Mills	St Michael's School, Somerville Road
Iron 'Scotch' Church	1–3 Old Christchurch Road
Town Hall Buildings	41–43 Old Christchurch Road
Criterion Arcade	The Arcade, 26–28 Old Christchurch Rd
Theatre Royale	Genting Casino, 9 Yelverton Road
Town Hall	Town Hall, Bourne Avenue
Sir Dan Godfrey	Hotel Collingwood, 11–13 Priory Road
First UK Municipal Beach Hut	Beach Hut, Undercliff Drive
Norfolk Royale	48 Richmond Hill
William Henry (WH) Smith	Walton House, 56–58 Richmond Hill
Granville Chambers	21 Richmond Hill
Hubert Parry	16 Richmond Hill
Lady Georgiana Fullerton	Sacred Heart Church, Richmond Hill
Lewis Tregonwell (Brown plaque)	Royal Exeter Hotel, Exeter Road
Town anti-pollution measures (Rectangular)	Flyover wall, Pier Approach

Walk 2

Bath Hotel	Royal Bath Hotel, Bath Road
J.R.R. Tolkien	Hotel Miramar, East Overcliff Drive
Flt Lt Jon Egging (RAF) (Brushed metal)	East Overcliff Drive
Stewart Granger	East Cliff Cottage Hotel, 57 Grove Road
Tony Hancock	Hotel Celebrity, 47 Gervis Road
Mary Shelley	St Peter's Road
Rupert Brooke (Stone plaque)	Dean Park Road
Downstairs Club	Holdenhurst Road
Christopher Crabb Creeke (Black plaque)	Holdenhurst Road
Metropole Hotel (Stone)	Lansdowne Crescent

Walk 3

Midland Hotel	Midland Heights, Norwich Avenue West

Walk 4

R.L. Stevenson (Brown plaque)	Alum Chine

Walk 5

Lillie Langtry	Langtry Manor Hotel, Derby Road
Sir Percy Florence Shelley	Shelley Manor, Beechwood Avenue
Stourfield House	Douglas Mews

Walk 6

Count Vladimir Chertkov	Former Iford Waterworks, Iford Lane

Walk 7

No plaques

Not seen on Walks

Inspector Frederick Abberline	195 Holdenhurst Road
Flora Thompson	4 Sedgley Road
Flora Thompson	2 Edgehill Road
Cecil Reginald Noble V.C.	175 Capstone Road
Frederick Charles Riggs V.C.	39 Capstone Road

Bibliography

Anderson, RC (1995) *Bournemouth and Poole Tramways*. Middleton Press, Midhurst.

Anonymous (1925–26) *A Pictorial and Descriptive Guide to Bournemouth*. Ward, Lock & Co, London.

Ashley, H (1985) *Explore Dorset*. Countryside Books, Newbury.

Bounds, J & Smith, D (2016) *Pier Review*. Summersdale Publishers, Chichester.

Butterworth N (2000) *Echoes of the Century: A Century of the Daily Echo* (Daily Echo Centenary 1900–2000). Newscom.

Christopher, J (2012) *Bournemouth through Time*. Amberley Publishing, Stroud.

Crane, N (2010) *Coast – Our Island Story*. BBC Books, London.

Crawford, A (1998) *Bournemouth*. The History Press, Stroud.

Davenport, M (1988) *Bygone Bournemouth*. Phillimore & Co, Chichester.

Edwards, E (1981) *A History of Bournemouth*. Phillimore & Co, Chichester.

Edwards, E (2006) *Famous Folk of Bournemouth, Poole and the Surrounding Area*. Natula Publications, Christchurch.

Edwards, J (2010) *A Bed by the Sea: A History of Bournemouth's Hotels*. Natula Publications, Christchurch.

Edwards, L & Treleven, J (2003) *The Definitive AFC Bournemouth*. Tony Brown, Beeston.

Emery, A (2008) *A History of Bournemouth Seafront*. The History Press, Stroud.

Fort, T (2015) *Channel Shore*. Simon & Schuster, London.

Gittings, R (1978) *Young Thomas Hardy*. Penguin Books, Harmondsworth.

Greenwood, D (1982) *Who's Buried where in England*. Constable & Company, London.

Guttridge, R (1986) *Dorset Murders*. Roy Gasson Associates, Wimborne.

Guttridge, R (1989) *Ten Dorset Mysteries*. Ensign Publications, Southampton.

Haag, M (2017) *The Durrells of Corfu*. Profile Books, London.

Hadfield, J (1973) *The Shell Guide to England*. Book Club Associates, London.

Hammond, RJW (1973) *Bournemouth and the New Forest*. Ward Lock, London.

Hatts, L (1985) *Exploring the Bournemouth Coast Path*. Countryside Books, Newbury.

Hoodless, WA (2012) *Bournemouth Curiosities*. The History Press, Stroud.

Kremer, J (2012) *Bournemouth A Go! Go! A Sixties Memoir*. Natula Publications, Christchurch.

Mate, CH (2014) *Bournemouth the Biography* (original 1910). Amberley Publishing, Stroud.

McKinstry, A (2015) *The Village of Tuckton 35,000 BC–1926*. Natula Publications, Christchurch.

Michelmore, C (1986) *Holidays by Rail in Great Britain*. David & Charles, Newton Abbot.

Mitchell, A (1999) *Memories of Bournemouth*. True North Books, Elland, West Yorkshire.

Mullay, AJ & M (2002) *The Book of British Birthplaces*. Breedon Books, Derby.

Needham, J (2010) *Bournemouth Past & Present*. The History Press, Stroud.

Needham, J (2012) *Bournemouth Then & Now*. The History Press, Stroud.

Needham, J (2015) *Bournemouth in the 1950s & '60s*. The History Press, Stroud.

Neesam, R (2005) *Champagne Cherries – A Season to Remember!* Robert Neesam.

Norman, A (2010) *Bournemouth's Founders and Famous Visitors*. The History Press, Stroud.

Oakley, M (2001) *Discover Dorset Railway Stations*. The Dovecote Press, Wimborne.

Perrin, L (2002) *A Century of Bournemouth*. Sutton Publishing, Stroud.

Popplewell, L (1973) *Bournemouth Railway History: An Exposure of Victorian Engineering Fraud*. Dorset Publishing Co, Wincanton.

Shakespeare, N (2017) *Six Minutes in May – How Churchill Unexpectedly Became Prime Minister*. Harvill Secker, London.

Skinner, J (2011) *Bournemouth. A Miscellany*. Identity Books.

Smith, C & Leslie W (1977) *Stories of Bournemouth and its Hinterland*. Privately published.

About the Author

Steve Roberts was born in Worcester in 1957 and brought up and educated in the Vale of Evesham. He completed teacher training in Birmingham, then taught in Brighton, Southend and Uxbridge, before moving to Bournemouth and marrying Val in 1984. He worked in IT for many years, becoming a project manager and Chartered Insurer. He set himself up as a freelance writer, public speaker and private tutor in 2012, and has had non-fiction articles published in over 75 different magazines. He has now written two books for Roving Press – *Lesser Known Christchurch* and *Lesser Known Bournemouth*.

www.steveroberts.org.uk
Twitter: @SRChristchurch

Some other books by Roving Press

If you enjoyed this book, why not try others in our range of local titles?

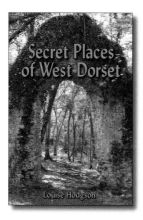

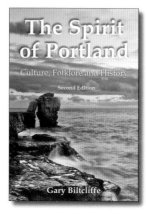

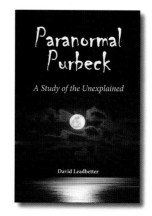

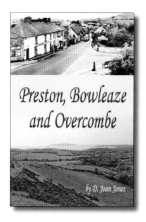

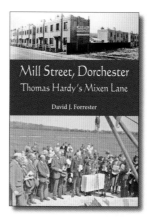

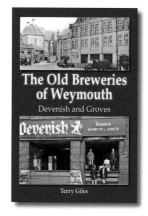

Roving Press

www.rovingpress.co.uk

If you like exploring, you'll love our books

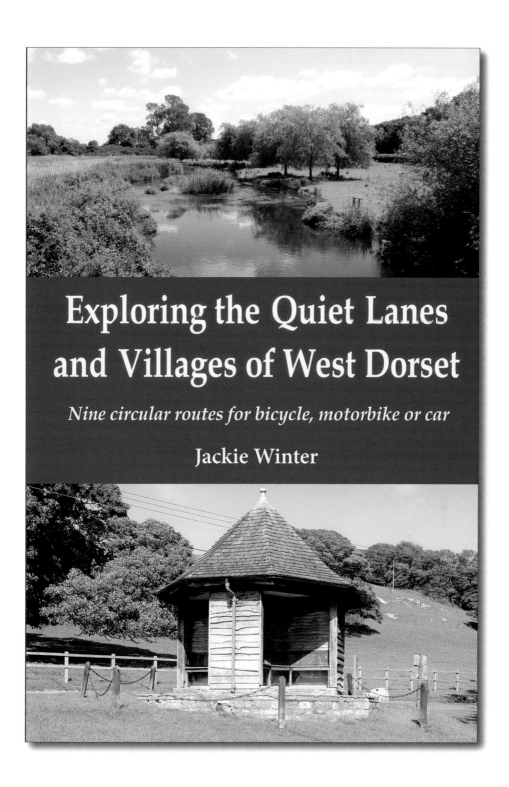

Exploring the Quiet Lanes and Villages of West Dorset

Nine circular routes for bicycle, motorbike or car

Jackie Winter

Index

Abberline, Frederick 67, 199
AFC Bournemouth 73, 80–81
AIDS wall 127
aviation (incl. Air Festival, air shows) 4,
  17, 19, 89, 95, 99, 102, 130, 157, 168–9,
  177, 190, 193
air-raid 19–20, 122, 133, 152
Alexander, Iain 47
alum 26–27
Alum Chine 8, 23, 26, 73, 137, 141, 151,
  197
Alum House 148
arcades,
  Bournemouth (Gervis/Henry Joy's/
    Royal) 12, 39, 98, 124
  Boscombe (Royal) 20, 108, 159
  Criterion 14, 124, 198
  Dalkeith 122
  Westbourne 12, 62, 63, 147–8, 153
archery 88
Argyll Gardens 39, 84, 89, 144
Argyll, Duke and Duchess 14, 150
Art and Makers Market 33, 92
Arts by the Sea Festival 95
Arts University Bournemouth 5, 17
athletics 20, 75, 86
aviary 33, 71, 125

B&DSME 73
Bournemouth and Boscombe Light Opera
  Company (BADS) 61
Bailey, Donald 20
bandstand 33, 37, 41, 51, 57, 102, 125,
  158
Barn Bight 170, 173
Barn Field 44
baseball 88
bathing machines 31
Bayly, Samuel 31
Bournemouth and Boscombe Light Opera
  Company (BBLOC) 59
beach huts 11, 31, 63, 126, 141, 155, 171,
  187, 198
Beale family 24, 37, 98–9,

Beales 4, 19, 58, 75, 98–9, 121
Bealesons 97, 99
Beardsley, Aubrey 46, 118, 156, 198
Beatles, the 54, 57–8
Bell Inn 41
Belle Vue Hotel 10, 105, 107, 117
Bennett, Morden 100–1, 135
Berry Hill 176, 177, 190
BH Live 5, 90
BH2 17, 74, 118, 125
Bournemouth International Centre (BIC)
  5–6, 12, 47, 49, 57, 59, 61, 87, 88, 89,
  127
Big Wheel 3, 72
Birch, Eugenius 12, 21
Black House 172
Blackburn, Tony 58, 116
Blind Man's Pond 38
Bournemouth Little Theatre Club (BLTC)
  61
Blue Flag award 23, 26, 29
Blunt, Anthony 69
BMX 75, 86, 87, 183
Bournemouth Natural Science Society
  (BNSS) 110
Bobby's 97
Boscombe Chine 27, 46, 49
Boscombe Chine Gardens 25, 40–1, 73,
  156, 158
Boscombe Cliff Gardens 40, 156
Boscombe Pier 14, 24, 37, 66, 72, 74, 78,
  89, 93, 96, 185
Bottomley, Horatio 19, 69
boundary line 18, 22, 27, 33, 41, 55, 141,
  153
Bourne Hall Hotel 115, 149
Bourne House 8, 123
Bourne, the (River/Stream) 1, 8, 22, 34,
  39, 48, 55, 106, 117, 123, 125
Bournemouth & Poole College 111, 132
Bournemouth 7s 92
Bournemouth Arts Club 47
Bournemouth Belle 16
Bournemouth Folk Club 59

Bournemouth Gardening Club 32
Bournemouth Pier 13, 68, 70, 71, 72,
    76–7, 87, 89, 93, 94, 125, 184
Bournemouth University 2, 4, 83, 193
Bowes, Mary 68
bowling 39, 41, 42, 57, 74, 84–5, 144
Boxer Rocket Shed 111
Branksome Arms 117
Branksome Dene Chine 24, 26, 68, 138,
    141
Branksome Towers 139
Brewster, Martyn 47
Bright's 97–8
Brompton Court 106, 123
Bronze Age 8, 44, 164, 190, 191
Brooke, Rupert 33, 51, 198
Bournemouth Symphony Orchestra
    (BSO) 56–7, 58
Burlington Mansions 157
Burton, John 14
buses 10, 17, 118, 119, 196

Cadena Café 118, 121
Cairns Memorial Hall 75, 129
Canford Heath 22, 184
Carlton Hotel 8, 20, 131
Castlepoint 4, 74, 183, 187, 197
Cemetery Junction 39
cenotaph 33, 123, 184
centenary 19, 34, 51, 124, 127, 168, 198
Central Gardens 22, 33, 73, 85, 96, 123,
    198
charabancs 16, 119
Charminster 32, 38, 39, 52, 87, 186–7,
    197
Cherries, the 17, 31, 80–1
Cherry Tree Walk 144
Chertkov, Vladimir 82, 164, 199
Chine Hotel 158
chines, geology and history 4, 24,
Chinese Giant 68–9
Christchurch Harbour 22, 79, 170, 187
Christmas 3, 37, 87, 89, 96, 98
churches,
    Christ Church 157
    Corpus Christi 160
    Holy Trinity 51, 69, 85, 103
    Iford URC 59
    Iron Scotch 118

Our Lady Immaculate 148
Pokesdown Congregational 191
Sacred Heart 50, 62, 120, 198
Spiritualist 131
St Ambrose 151, 152
St Andrew's URC 83, 103, 118, 122
St Andrews (Kinson) 8, 65, 112
St Clement's 100, 102, 112
St James (Pokesdown) 191
St John's (Boscombe) 80, 158
St John's (Holdenhurst) 112, 182
St Katharine's 192
St Mark's 193
St Michael's 112, 116
St Peter's 10, 48, 49, 55, 56, 100–2, 112,
    135, 138
St Stephen's 100, 101, 102, 112, 123
St Swithun's 51
Wesleyan Methodist 149
West Cliff Baptist 149
Churchill, Winston 26, 125, 138, 142
cinemas 61, 63–4, 117, 121, 124, 125, 129,
    147, 149
coaches 16, 196
Coastal Activity Park 74, 79
Coastwatch 170–1
coat of arms 7, 160
College of Chiropractic 160
Collegiate School 104, 160
Colosseum 63–4, 147
Constitutional Club 112, 120
Cooper-Dean 8, 27, 80, 141, 151, 189,
copperas 8, 26, 161
Corbin, Bob 81
County Gates 27, 139, 153
Court Royal 127, 198
Cox, Sam 2
Coy Pond 22, 184
Crabb Creeke, Christopher 12, 47, 106,
    112, 127, 161, 193, 198
Crescent, the 158
cricket 12, 37, 82–3, 90,
Cricketers Arms 186
croquet 39, 89
cruises, steamship 10, 13, 27
Cutler, Joseph 27
cycling 43, 86–7, 184–185

Dalkeith Chambers 122

darts 88
Darwin, Charles 49, 141
Day, Robert 12
D-Day 20, 53, 105, 138
Dean Park 12, 82–3, 86, 88, 89
Debenhams 97
Decoy Pond 8, 35, 123
Digby Chambers 119
Dingles 39, 97
doggers 171, 173
Double Dykes 19, 44, 168, 170, 172
Downstairs Club 57, 133, 198
Drummond Wolff, Henry 24, 47, 69, 157,
    158, 161
Durley Chine 27, 66, 78, 79, 80, 141–2
Durrell family 52, 187

East Cliff Lift 11, 18, 30–1, 47, 130
Echo, the 17, 55, 62, 103, 121, 122, 185
Egging, Jon 130, 177, 198
electric lighting 12, 125, 126, 180
Elliott, Thomas 16
Emery, Andrew 20, 54, 63
Ensbury, 22, 74, 75, 83, 86, 87, 89, 190–1,
    193, 197
Eurostay Hotel 115
Evans, Chris 35

Fairmount Hotel 115
Falaise 144
Fampoux Gardens 42
Fern Bank 122
ferries 71, 166–167, 173, 187, 191, 193
Ferry, Benjamin 10, 112
fire station 2–3, 15, 59, 63, 133, 152
Fisherman's Walk 20, 23, 24, 29, 30, 41,
    57, 73, 93, 160
Fisherman's Walk Cliff Lift 192
fishing 8, 24, 39, 41, 79–80, 190
Fitzgerald, F.R. 47
flying *see* aviation
Food and Drink Festival 92
Fortes 117, 132
Foy, Jeremy 30

Gilbert and Sullivan Productions (GASP)
    59
Gaumont 57–8, 125, 129
gay scene 117

Geneen, Harold Sydney 18
geology 39, 110
Gervis Place 97, 98, 119, 124, 196
Goat & Tricycle 116
Godfrey, Dan 56, 115, 198
golf 37, 38, 74, 83–4, 90, 163, 184
Goodall, Jane 54, 62
Grand Hotel 134
Grand Theatre 65, 108, 159
Granville Chambers 122, 198
Great Train Robbers 70
Green Flag award 33, 43, 91
Grove, the 11, 131
Gulliver, Isaac 8, 42, 188
Gulliver's Tavern 65, 188
Gulliver's Trail 43

Hahnemann House 116
Haig, Henry 13
Halo nightclub 118
Hamel, Gustav 37
Hamilton Court House 148
Hampshire Centre 4
Hampshire Court 123
Hancock, Tony 58, 62, 131, 198
Happylands Arcade 31
Hardy, Thomas 50, 181
Harvey, Tom 167
Heath, Neville 68, 143
Hemingway, Wayne and Gerardine 21,
    28, 155
Hengistbury Head 1, 8, 19, 23, 24, 44–5,
    65, 71, 72, 79, 83, 163, 168–71, 178,
    184, 185, 193–5
Herbert Hospital 151
Herz, Cornelius 69
Hesketh, Richard 44
Hicks Farm 178
Highcliff Hotel 19, 51, 147
Highcliffe Castle 80, 172, 194
hockey 88, 89, 92
Holburn, Rory 76
Holdenhurst 8, 15, 18, 22, 112, 178–83,
    184, 189, 190
Holloway's Dock 173
Honeycombe Chine 47, 155, 156
horse racing 191
Horseshoe Common 33, 38, 133
Hot Rocks 127

Hotel Celebrity 131, 198
Hotel Collingwood 115, 198
Hotel Miramar 53, 105, 130, 198
Howard, Brenden 11
Howarth, Maggy 48, 118
Hurn 22, 49, 82, 181, 196

ice skating 3, 33, 89, 96, 124, 125
Iford 8, 43, 66, 67, 73, 78, 79, 82, 87, 88,
    112, 184, 187–8, 193, 199
IMAX 17, 62, 126
Invalids' Walk 10, 32, 125
Iron Age 8, 44, 168, 193
Irving, Henry 59, 161, 197

J.J. Allen 52, 97–8, 135, 148, 149
Jacey House 132
James Fisher Medical Centre 13
Jewish connections 54, 138, 150
Joseph's Steps 27, 142
Joy, Henry 12, 39, 124, 147

Karabits, Kirill 56
Kelly, Fiona 47
Kemp-Welch, Lucy 46
Kids Free Fun Festival 33
Kingfisher Barn Visitor Centre 22, 43,
    176, 178, 184
Kings Park 20, 37, 43, 73, 75, 80, 82, 84,
    86
Kings Park Nursery 35–6
Kinson 8–9, 18, 42, 65, 73, 76, 82, 84, 85,
    87, 112, 188–9, 197
Kirkby, Andy 161
Knole, the 111
Knyveton Gardens 41, 84, 85

Lacey, Frederick 37
land train 40, 72–3, 145, 163, 173
Laney, F.E. 14
Langtry, Lillie and Manor 20, 59, 65–6,
    199
language schools 3, 5, 153
Lansdowne 12, 19, 111, 132–3, 198
Lawrence, D.H. 51, 104, 135
libraries 10, 107, 111, 117, 133, 148, 164,
    186, 187, 195, 197
lifeboat 15, 93
lifeguards 30, 141–2, 197

candlelight illuminations 33, 94
lions 48, 123
Littledown 43, 73, 74, 75, 82, 87, 88,
    90–1, 112, 133, 189–90
Longham 8, 52, 65, 79, 112
Lower Gardens 3, 10, 18, 21, 22, 32, 33,
    36, 51, 55, 57, 71, 74, 88, 89, 92, 94, 96,
    119, 125
LV=KidZone 29

MacGregor, John 79
Malmesbury, Earls of 49, 179, 181, 186
Manchester Hotel 116
marathon 92, 96
Marconi, Guglielmo 18, 127, 198
Marriott Highcliff 142
Marsham Court Hotel 129–30, 131
Mary Shelley pub 97, 135
Mercury House 135
Messenger, Geoff 90
Metropole Hotel 19, 132, 198
Meyrick Park 16, 18, 33, 37, 83, 84, 85,
    88, 89, 184
Meyrick Steps 31
Meyrick, George 37
Midland Heights 150, 199
Mighty Claws 74
Miles, Hattie 185
Millhams Mead 43, 79
Mills, Freddie 88–9, 116, 198
miniature railway 73, 189
minigolf 33, 41, 74, 126
Mont Dore Hotel 14, 65, 99, 106–7, 123
Moordown 8, 18, 70, 73, 76, 84, 85, 195
Moore Avenue Park 42, 74
Motabitz 160
Mr Mulligans 74
Muccleshell 177–8, 190
Mudeford 15, 71, 73, 163, 171, 173, 195
mural 47, 48, 127, 133, 141
Muscliff 13, 22, 43, 74, 82, 85, 112, 175–7,
    190

Nash, Paul 47
Nash, Eustace 46, 88
nature reserves 22, 32, 37, 39, 40, 42, 43,
    44, 79, 138, 163, 176, 177, 184
Neolithic Age 8
Norfolk Royale Hotel 120, 198

O2 Academy 59, 65, 108, 159
Oakmeadians 37, 88
Oasis Fun 74, 85
Obscura Café 118
Oceanarium 72, 78, 127
Odeon 17, 58, 63, 74, 118, 124, 125
Outdoor Education Centre (OEC) 79,
    168
Old Forest Lodge 131
Old Lodge 137
Old Waterworks 164, 199
Overcliff Nature Reserve 40
Overstrand, the 21, 28, 155

Packe Family Mausoleum 139
Palmerston Arms 159
Pantechnicon 148
Park Central Hotel 127
Parker, Henry Perlee 9, 46
Parry, Hubert 50, 57, 120, 198
Pavilion 5, 33, 57, 59, 61, 89, 107–8, 125
Pavilion Dance South West 61
Pelhams Park 42, 74, 82, 84, 85, 87, 90,
    189
pergola 35, 124, 198
pétanque 85
Pier Approach 1, 10, 12, 18, 28, 72, 74, 87,
    126, 127, 196, 198
Pig Shoot 179
Piggery 178
pine trees 9, 10, 33, 48, 193
Pine Walk 10, 32, 33, 47, 71, 92, 102, 125
Playgolf 74, 83
Plummer Roddis 97, 119
Pokesdown 8, 15, 18, 41, 48, 75, 76, 84,
    85, 99, 100, 159, 180, 187, 191, 196, 197
police station 14, 20, 133
Poole Bay 1, 20, 23, 27, 28, 30, 70, 105,
    139
Poole Hill Brewery 116
Poppies, the 81–2
Portillo, Michael 31, 63, 105
Portman Lodge 10, 160
post office 10, 15, 119, 133, 148, 180
powerboating 71, 79
Pride Festival 93
Proctor, Philip 60
Profumo affair 69–70
Pug's Hole 37, 184

Quarry Pond 171
Queens Park 33, 38, 74, 83, 87, 88, 90,
    187
Queens Park Improvement and
    Protection Society (QUIPS) 38

racketball 85
radio 18, 59
railway stations, 15–16, 31, 41, 55, 63, 68,
    99–100, 105, 150, 186, 191, 194, 196
Rattenbury murder 62, 66, 68
reading rooms 10, 107
Red Arrows 95, 130, 177
Redhill 42, 74, 84, 85, 191
regattas 78, 93, 94
Rennie, George 13
Richmond Hill 12, 16, 49, 50, 52, 57, 62,
    68, 83, 103, 112, 118, 120, 122, 129, 198
River Stour 22–3, 43, 66, 67, 71, 78, 83,
    164, 166–7, 172, 178, 179, 185, 187,
    190, 191, 193
Riverside, the 166
RNLI see lifeboat and lifeguards
rock garden, Pavilion 33, 125
RockReef 77
Roddis House 97, 119
roller skating 14, 89
Rolls, Charles 168–9
Roundhouse 132
rowing 78, 79, 93
Royal Bath Hotel 10, 20, 50, 53, 59, 110,
    129, 181, 198
Royal London House 132
Royal National Sanatorium 10, 11, 106,
    123
Royal Victoria apartments 150
royal visits 20
Royal Exeter Hotel 1, 10, 104, 112, 115,
    127, 198
rugby 37, 88, 92
Russell-Cotes, 20, 47, 55, 59, 62, 88, 104,
    108–10, 130, 197
Russian colony 82, 164–5, 187
Rustic Bridge 55, 124

sailing 27, 79, 93
San Remo Towers 156
sand sculptures 31
Schillig, Guido 5

Scott, Elisabeth 112
scouts 68, 75–6, 195
Seafield Gardens 41, 74, 84, 85
seafront rangers 29
Sedding, J.D. 102, 111
Selfie Wall Trail 47, 141
Selfridge, Harry 80, 194
Sells, Jonathan 47
Shake & Stir Vintage Festival 93
Sheepwash 43
Shelley Manor, Theatre and Medical
    Centre 59, 60–1, 63, 65, 70, 161
Shelley family 14, 36, 40, 48–9, 60–1, 102,
    135, 159, 161, 198, 199
Shelley Park 40, 85, 161
shooting 88
Sir David English Sports Centre 82, 89,
    90
skate parks 75, 87
Skerryvore 21, 50, 151, 152
Slade, Darren 17
Slades Farm 74, 75, 82, 86, 87
Smith, Archibald 13, 14
Solent Meads 44, 83
Southbourne 18, 19, 24, 28, 29, 39, 41, 50,
    52, 54, 58, 62, 67, 68, 73, 74, 76, 80, 84,
    85, 93, 111, 192, 197
Southbourne Pier 13, 79,
Southbourne Terrace 119
Sovereign Centre 34, 160
Springbourne 2, 18, 47, 62, 74, 159, 186,
    197
Square, the 8, 19, 22, 33, 48, 92, 97,
    117–18, 123–4
squash 85, 91
St Michael's School 88, 116, 198
Stable, the 124
Stevenson, R.L. 21, 46, 50–1, 137, 144,
    151, 152, 161, 199
Stour Valley Nature Reserve 22, 43, 79,
    176
Stour Valley Way 172, 184
Stourfield Chase 8, 192
Stourfield House 66, 68, 70, 191, 192, 199
Street Food Corner 33
Strouden 8, 42, 82, 187
students 2, 5, 111, 115, 124, 133, 135
Suchomlin, John 31
Supermarine Aviation 27

Surf Boat Club 78
surfing 28, 78–9, 140, 155
swimming 87, 90, 93, 96
Sydenham, John 10, 55, 107

Talbot Woods 65, 70, 91, 190, 193
Tapps Arms 9, 119
Tapps family 9, 10, 120, 183, 184
Taylor, Isaac 8, 45
telephone exchange 131, 152
tennis 33, 39, 41, 73, 85, 91, 105, 158, 161
Terry, Ian 101
Theatre Royal 14, 50, 121, 122, 198
Thompson, Flora 51, 195, 199
Throop 22, 23, 66, 112, 175–80, 184, 190
Titanic survivor 69
Tolkien, J.R.R. 53, 105, 130, 138, 140, 198
toll house 166, 188
Tollard Royal Hotel 63, 68, 143
Tolstoy, Leo 82, 164–5, 187
town hall 14, 19, 47, 48, 65, 106–7, 121,
    123, 124, 198
trams 16, 118, 123, 133–4, 153, 166, 188,
    195
Tregonwell Arms 9, 15, 119,
Tregonwell, Lewis 1, 9–10, 47, 104, 106,
    115, 127, 135, 198
Triangle, the 76, 88, 117, 197
trolley-buses 16
Trouville Hotel 115
Tuckton 19, 23, 43, 52, 68, 70, 71, 74, 78,
    82, 164–8, 173, 184, 187–8, 193, 197
turbary 37
Turbary Common 42
Turner, Steve 5
twinning 4, 5, 123

Undercliff Cloisters 126
Undercliff, the 13, 18, 109, 126, 192
Upper Gardens 8, 22, 33, 34–5, 83, 184

Valiente, Doreen 69
Viewpoint House 138
Vintage Lounge 63, 147
Vitality stadium 3, 80

WH Smith 15, 119, 122, 198
Walker, Duncan 109
Walton House 122, 198

Ward, Moffat 47
Warren Hill 169, 170
water polo 87, 93
water tower 34–5, 37, 41
Weaver, Jon 3
Wentworth House 160
Wessex Christian Centre 61, 129
Wessex Way/A338/Spur Road 22, 38, 133, 183, 184, 186, 190
West Cliff Green 143
West Cliff Lift 18, 27, 142
West Hants Club 85, 91
West Moors 9
Westover Gardens 32, 124
whale 14, 66
Whitehouse, Paul 63
Wick 44–5, 70, 71, 79, 112, 163–4, 167, 173, 193
Wilde, Oscar 50, 104
Wilkes Booth, John and Asia 67
Wimborne Road Cemetery 39, 51, 67, 69, 79
Winter Gardens 17, 50, 57, 58, 69, 84, 88, 89, 115
Winton 18, 42, 52, 61, 65, 74, 75, 76, 81, 82, 84, 85, 194–5, 197
Woodland Walk 160, 184

YMCA 75, 129
youth centres 75–6

Zetland Court 138, 152
zig-zags, 27, 29, 31, 130, 142, 145, 155
zip-wire 33, 77, 75